THE DISTRIBUTION AND
REDISTRIBUTION OF INCOMES

OCCASIONAL PAPERS ON SOCIAL ADMINISTRATION NO. 67

Editorial Committee under the
Chairmanship of Professor Brian Abel-Smith
London School of Economics and Political Science

D0259941

Related titles in the Occasional Papers series
available from Bedford Square Press:

The Poor and the Poorest   Brian Abel-Smith and Peter Townsend
Income Redistribution and the Welfare State   Adrian Webb and Jack Sieve
Administrative Justice and Supplementary Benefits   Melvin Herman
Public Assistance in France   Cindy Stevens
French Pensions   Tony Lynes
Large Families in London   Hilary Land
Supplementary Benefits and the Consumer   Eric Briggs and Anthony Rees
In Search of the Scrounger   Alan Deacon
Child Support in the European Community
                              Jonathan Bradshaw and David Piachaud

Other recent titles in the series:

Unmet Needs and the Delivery of Care   Paul Chapman
Aids and Adaptations   Ursula Keeble
Allocating the Home Help Services
                      Neil Howell, Duncan Boldy and Barry Smith
How Many Patients?   John Butler

THE DISTRIBUTION AND REDISTRIBUTION OF INCOMES

David Piachaud
with an appendix by Tony Cornford

BEDFORD SQUARE PRESS of the
National Council for Voluntary Organisations

First published 1982 by the
Bedford Square Press of the
National Council for Voluntary Organisations
26 Bedford Square,
London WC1B 3HU

© 1982 Social Administration Research Trust

ISBN 0 7199 1086 2

Printed in Great Britain by
Imediaprint Limited

FOREWORD

This series of Occasional Papers was started in 1960 to supply the
need for a medium of publication for studies in the field of social
policy and administration which fell between the two extremes of
the short article and the full-length book. Since the inception
of this series of papers, it has, however, been extended to include
many which might better be described as books: comparative speed of
publication being one factor that has attracted authors to us. It
was thought that such a series would not only meet a need among
research workers and writers concerned with contemporary social
issues, but would also strengthen links between students of the
subject and administrators, social workers, committee members and
others with responsibilities and interest in the social services.

Contributions to the series are welcome from any source and should
be submitted in the first instance to the Secretary, Social
Administration Research Trust at the London School of Economics.
The series is now published by the Bedford Square Press to which
all queries about this and previous titles should be addressed.

Acknowledgements

It would be surprising if any of the people who responded to the survey on which this study is based were to read this, but without them there could be no study.   The Department of Employment gave permission to use the data from the Family Expenditure Survey and M.J. Reeves and R.U. Redpath gave helpful comments.   The SSRC Survey Archive supplied the data and Eric Roughley was unfailingly helpful.

The computing could not have been carried out but for the great skill and patient explanations of Tony Cornford.   Other help with computing was given by Steven Barnes, Tomoko Barker and Wiji Narendranathan.

Richard Layard provided the stimulus, without which the study would never have been started or finished, and many helpful comments.   Other advice, comments and encouragement were received from, among others, Brian Abel-Smith, Mike Reddin, Jon Stern, Toni Zabalza and Sally Baldwin.

Typing was carried out most accurately and cheerfully by Bettie Jory, Pam Mounsey, Lorraine Kuhne and Phyllis Gamble.

The SSRC provided financial support to the Centre for Labour Economics for a study of income distribution and labour supply of which this forms a part.

None of those mentioned is responsible in any way for this analysis, its interpretation or its shortcomings.   But to all of them sincere thanks are offered.

CONTENTS

Chapter 1

Introduction

The purpose of this study is, first, to describe the distribution of incomes in Britain and, second, to simulate and compare the redistributive effects of a range of possible policies designed to alter the distribution of incomes and reduce the extent of poverty.

The study is based on the Family Expenditure Survey (FES) of 1977; this survey was carried out by the Office of Population Censuses and Surveys on behalf of the Department of Employment. Data which was altogether anonymous was made available through the SSRC Survey Archive. Survey data has been used to describe the distribution of incomes and the survey respondents are treated as a representative sample with which the overall effects of policy changes may be simulated.

The scope and structure of the study may best be indicated by outlining the contents of this paper.

In this introduction previous work on income distribution and on policy simulations is discussed; definitions of income, the nature of the FES data, alternative methods of describing inequalities and the simulations are then considered. Part I attempts to describe the distribution of incomes: first, in relation to general and personal characteristics; second, in relation to status in the labour market; and third, in relation to incomes from social security. This first part is provided both for its own sake and as necessary background for the second part. In Part II a variety of policies are simulated. In Chapter 5, the possible effects of a minimum wage law are assessed. In Chapters 6 and 7 a variety of possible changes in support for children and elderly people are considered. In Chapter 8 the distributional effects of alternative methods of financing increased benefits are considered and various forms of tax credit and negative income tax are discussed. In Chapter 9, some combined, self-financing combinations of policy changes are considered. Finally, the results are discussed and some conclusions are drawn.

Background to the study

There is a long tradition of literature in Britain concerned with poverty and the distribution of incomes. This dates back to the work of Booth and Rowntree on poverty in London and York but it is only in the post-war period that extensive data has been available to analyse incomes on a national basis including all income levels. One of the most important studies of this kind was that of Abel-Smith and Townsend, The Poor and the Poorest (1965); their study was, like the present one, based on data from the Family Expenditure Surveys, in their case for the years 1953-54 and 1960. A more recent study using the 1971 Family Expenditure Survey was that of Fiegehen et.al. (1977) which investigated, among other things, the life-cycle and expenditure patterns. A different data source, the General Household Survey, was used in a study of The Causes of Poverty by Layard et.al. (1978) which placed particular emphasis on the relationship between the distribution of incomes and the labour market. The only major study in recent years not to be based on secondary analysis of data collected by government departments is that of Townsend (1979) which investigated in particular the concept of relative deprivation.

All these studies have been drawn on heavily in formulating the concepts and questions examined in this study.

While there have been many studies describing and analysing the distribution of incomes there have been relatively few which analysed the possible effects of changes in policy. Brown (1972), for example, analysed the effects of Budget changes but when this study was carried out FES data was only available in the form of tables based on grouped data. It is only in recent years that individual data, in an anonymous form to safeguard respondents' identities, became available to researchers through the SSRC Survey Archive. This data has been used in studies of income distribution and to analyse the effects of particular policies. It has not been used to compare a broad range of alternative policies.

This study therefore uses data that is more recent than that used in any of the studies mentioned and, by treating the FES data on individual families as a representative sample of the population, provides simulations of the effects of policy changes.

Data and definitions ✝

The analysis of the distribution of incomes requires definition of three elements:

a)   The income unit to be considered.

b)   The time period over which income is to be measured.

c)   The measure of income level.

Each of these elements will be considered in turn:

a)   The income unit

The income unit used as the basis for most of the analysis presented here is the inner family - a lone person or a couple plus dependent children. Children who are economically active are treated as separate family units even though they may be living with their parent(s).   This unit is used for two reasons: i) Most policies operate at the level of such units. ii) Even if several such units live together it is now generally assumed that such units should be able to be self-supporting. Here this unit is always referred to as the "family".

For some purposes, however, income has been considered both in relation to the family (as just defined) and also in relation to the household (defined in terms of people living together).

Relevant data was extracted by the SSRC Survey Archive for all individuals included in the survey.   From this individual data families were "constituted". This process was complex involving the processing of each individual within each household to examine which family unit they belonged to and determining whether or not children were to be treated as dependent or independent. A considerable amount of the FES data is collected only on the household basis and this had to be allocated between families. For example in the case of housing expenditure the proportion payable by each family had to be estimated: this was done in proportion to the gross income of each family unit within the household. (For about two-thirds of families no difficulty arose since the household consisted of only one family.) Having "constituted" the family it was necessary to combine the very many different possible sources of income to produce income aggregates.

Families were for purposes of analysis divided into 12 family types:

Elderly Couple	- Couple, man aged over 65 (in a very few cases with children)
Elderly Man	- Lone man aged over 65
Elderly Woman	- Lone woman aged over 60
Couple, No children	- Head not aged over 65
Couple, 1 child	- Head not aged over 65
Couple, 2 children	- Head not aged over 65
Couple 3 children	- Head not aged over 65
Couple, 4 children	- Head not aged over 65
Couple, 5+ children	- Head not aged over 65
Lone Parent, 1+ child	- Head not aged over 60 (woman) or 65 (man)
Single man	- Lone man (single, widowed, divorced or separated) not aged over 65
Single woman	- Lone woman (single, widowed, divorced or separated) not aged over 60

b) The time period

Income fluctuates for many people from week to week and month to month. The analysis here is primarily based on the earnings defined by survey respondents

as "usual", or normal.   For most people this is close to their current earnings
at the time of interview.   There is, however, one important feature of the
definition of normal income used by the Family Expenditure Survey: employees who
have been away from work due to sickness or unemployment for 13 weeks or less
are regarded, for the purposes of defining normal income, as continuing to receive
their normal earnings and short-term social security benefits are not included in
their normal income.

c)   The measure of income level

The measure of income level used in most of this study is:

> Gross money income
>
> less : Direct taxes
>
> less : Housing costs
>
> as a proportion of : Supplementary Benefit personal requirements.

The purpose of this definition is to measure net income relative to needs.
This definition corresponds with that used in Layard et.al. (1978), where it is
extensively discussed.   The scale of needs that has been used is the Supplementary
Benefit (SB) scale rates for long-term recipients applicable at the time of
interview.   Supplementary benefit rates have been used because they represent an
official definition of minimum requirements.   The long-term rate is used because
the analysis is, for the most part, concerned with normal incomes out of which
families have to meet all their needs over long periods of time.

The SB scale rates applicable for most of 1977 were:

Single person		£15.70 per week
Married couple		£24.85 per week
Child Aged :	Under 5	£3.60 per week
	5-10	£4.35 per week
	11-12	£5.35 per week
	13-15	£6.50 per week
	16-17	£7.80 per week.

Where household income levels are considered they are based on the sum of family incomes in the household relative to the sum of family SB levels in the household. (The latter differs from the level that would be assessed by supplementary benefits if the household were treated as one unit; the procedure followed here is to ensure that possible transfers within households, which are discussed below, sum to zero).

The computational methodology in preparing the data for analysis is explained and discussed in Appendix 1. The computer programme used to construct income and other variables is reproduced in Appendix 2.

The analysis in the study is based on 9152 families containing 19697 individuals.

Certain features of the survey affect its usefulness and reliability for analysing the distribution of incomes and for policy simulations.

a) There are limitations on data collected although the FES income data is very detailed and in most respects far superior to the General Household Survey. The most serious gaps from economic and social perspectives are the lack of data on educational and employment history.

b) There are limitations since one-third of those sampled are non-respondents. This biases the results to some extent although the overall problem may not be very great. A particular problem arises with certain sources of income which may be seriously understated; this is a particular problem with the self-employed. Since problems of response have been extensively discussed elsewhere (for example by Kemsley et al, 1980) it will not be considered further here. The bold assumption is made that the sample is representative of the British population.

c) There are limitations since, inevitably, the data available is out of date. With stable prices and incomes this would present no great difficulty. With rapid inflation, results presented using data four years out of date (as those presented here) carry little meaning when expressed in current prices. It is therefore necessary either to adjust money values to current price levels - which will soon lose meaning with further inflation - or express values in relation to mean values or some reasonably constant reference level. The latter approach is adopted, using SB levels which currently (1981) have very nearly the same real value as in 1977.

Descriptions of Distributions

In describing the distribution of incomes of over 9,000 families some summary statistics are clearly essential to indicate the degree of equality or inequality. Here a number of alternative indicators are used.

First, the proportions of families in different ranges of income levels are presented. Second, percentiles (5th, 10th, 25th, 50th, 75th, 90th and 95th) are shown. Third, the Gini coefficient has been computed; broadly speaking, the higher this is, the greater the degree of inequality. Fourth, the Atkinson measure of equality has been used. This is defined as:

$$E = \frac{\left(\overline{y^{\alpha}}\right)^{\frac{1}{\alpha}}}{\overline{y}}$$

The parameter alpha represents the weight attached by society to inequality in the distribution: here values of -0.5, -1.0 and -2.0 have been used. The higher the value of the Atkinson measure, the greater the degree of equality. This measure is conceptually most satisfactory, even if it is the most complex and difficult to interpret.

It is not the purpose here to explore the properties of these alternative statistics (which is done in, for example, Atkinson, 1970); rather the purpose is to use them.

The Simulations

The simulations carried out are described in detail in Part II.   There are however a number of general points relating to the simulations which may conveniently be made here.

The range of possible policies that could be simulated is infinite; some selection had to be made. Three criteria were used.   First, the concern was with policies of most direct relevance to those at low income levels.   Second, only policies that had been extensively advocated were considered.   Third, policies for which the data was ill-suited were excluded: these included changes in short-term and means-tested benefits and changes in the level of unemployment.

The simulations have been carried out on a discrete basis.   Effects on individuals are estimated and aggregated for the family.   While any increase in income is, in some cases, made subject to income tax, it has been assumed there are no repercussions on other benefits.   This is a major simplification but it was judged necessary to limit complications and avoid obfuscations.

Changes in policies may have significant labour supply effects.   The purpose here is not to investigate such effects but possible effects must be taken into account in considering the redistributive impact of policies.   Where possible, estimates of labour supply effects have been incorporated.   In other cases the effects of purely illustrative labour supply effects have been analysed.   In yet other cases, where there is little or no knowledge of possible labour supply effects, it has been assumed there are no such effects.

Presentation

This study is essentially quantitative; for this reason the results are for the most part contained and presented in the form of tables.   The main features of the results are described in the text but no attempt has been made to repeat all the results contained in the tables in the text - to do so would serve little purpose and would be extremely boring.

PART I - DESCRIPTION

Chapter 2

The Distribution of Incomes

The purpose of this chapter is to describe the distribution of incomes in relation to general and personal characteristics; the labour market and social security are specifically considered n the following chapters.

The distribution of income levels by type of family is shown in Table 2.1. Overall 6.4 per cent of families were below 90 per cent of SB level and a further 4.7 per cent were between 90 and 100 per cent of SB level. Considering individuals, 5.1 per cent were in families that were below 90 per cent of SB level with another 3.7 per cent between 90 and 100 per cent of SB level. The proportion under SB level varied from 3.5 per cent of non-elderly childless couples to 32.9 per cent of lone parents with children.

The composition of different income levels is shown in Table 2.2: elderly families, which constituted 22.8 per cent of all families, made up 26.1 per cent of those under 90 per cent of SB level and 57.1 per cent of those between 90 and 100 per cent of SB level; single people were disproportionately represented in the lowest income level and childless couples in the highest income levels.

The distribution of individuals based on their family income is shown in Table 2.3. When individuals rather than families are considered the larger families are of course of more significance: couples with 3 or more children represented only 4.1 per cent of all families below 90 per cent of SB level but they include 14.1 per cent of the individuals below this level.

The analysis in Tables 2.1 to 2.3 is based on the family's normal income. It is also of interest to consider the household circumstances of these families First the extent to which families were in shared, multi-family households may be considered, as shown in Table 2.4. (It should be reiterated that the family units within a household may be directly related). Overall 39 per cent of families were sharing but this proportion varied greatly from under one-fifth of

larger families to over three-quarters of non-elderly single people.   There was
no clear relationship with income level although those in the lowest income level
shared more than on average.   The extent of sharing is clearly of relevance to
the relationship between family and household income but it gives no indication
of the extent to which families may gain or lose from their common household.

To estimate the possible, although not necessarily actual, transfer within
households a statistic for the mean implicit transfer within the household,
MTRANS, has been defined as follows:

$$\text{MTRANS} = \text{MY} . \frac{\text{FSB}}{\text{MSB}} - \text{FY}$$

where MY and FY are the household and family net income respectively

and MSB and FSB are the household and family SB level respectively.

On the assumption that income is shared within the household, MTRANS indicates
what would have to be passed to (or from) a family unit from (or to) other members
of the household in order to raise (or lower) the family's income level to that
of the household in which they live.   The mean values of this implicit transfer
are shown in Table 2.4; the elderly, lone parents and single people are, or could
be, the principal gainers from such transfers; those at low-family income levels
gain at the expense of higher income levels - not surprisingly since the implicit
transfer is a notional equalisation within households.   It must be stressed that
this transfer and equalisation may or may not take place; adequate information to
determine the extent of redistribution within multi-family households would be
extremely complex and simply does not exist.

The distribution of families based on household income (implicitly assuming
the transfer discussed above does take place) is shown in Table 2.5.   Overall,
the proportion of families under SB level falls from 11.1 per cent based on family
income (Table 2.1) to 7.4 percent based on household income.   The most dramatic

difference occurs with single people of whom the proportion under SB level based on household income is less than half that based on family income.

The analysis thus far has been based on "normal" income - as is most of this study. In Table 2.6 the relationship between normal and current income levels is analysed; it is clear that there is a wider disparity of incomes over a shorter time period than over a longer time period. (The data make it impossible to go beyond normal income to any estimate of life-time income).

The various alternative measures of income are summarised using the measures of distribution discussed in the introduction in Table 2.7. It is clear, using the Gini coefficient or Atkinson measures, that the inequality of incomes relative to SB level (or income levels for short) is less than that of net incomes. It is also clear that the distribution of families by normal income level is more equal than by current income level, and by household income is more equal than by family income.

Variations in income by sex and by age are considered in Table 2.8-2.11. Shifts in type of family, income level and economic status are presented for men and women in Tables 2.8 and 2.9; the content of each of these tables is self-explanatory but a few contrasts between them are of interest. Men marry later than women but a far higher proportion have ended their days as part of a couple. Women's family income levels are on average lower than men's and this is particularly marked in the older age groups. (This assumes pooling of income within families; no account is taken of inequalities in income distribution within the family. This assumption is clearly unjustifiable but there is no data on which to make any better estimates.) The most marked difference lies, not surprisingly, in economic status.

To some extent the life-cycle shown by this cross-sectional profile differs from Rowntree's life cycle. The middle years when children are present does not, on average, represent a period of hardship; this is in part attributable to smaller families and in part to the growth of paid work of married women.

The extent of shared households and of low income levels based on both family and household incomes are shown for men and women in Tables 2.10 and 2.11. A higher proportion of women than of men were in shared households; younger men were

more likely to be sharing and older men less likely than women of the same age.
It is among those under 21 who are most likely to be sharing, in many cases with
their parents, that there is the greatest difference between the extent of low
income levels as measured by family and household income - a difference between
20.8 per cent and 2.6 per cent below SB level based on family and household income
respectively for men under 18.

Income has been used throughout this study as a measure of command over
resources. It has many deficiencies one of which is that it gives no direct
indication of the ownership of capital assets that affect opportunities and living
standards. Townsend (1979), among others, has emphasised the importance of
wealth in assessing inequalities. While there is no attempt here to estimate
levels of wealth and relate these to, or incorporate them in, measures of income,
two types of capital assets - housing and consumer durables - are considered in
relation to income levels.

Housing tenure by type of family and income level is shown in Table 2.12;
the most marked features are the extent to which the elderly live in housing
owned outright and to which lone parents and single people live in rented
accommodation. Owner-occuption increases with income level but striking
proportions of those in the lowest income levels own their housing outright or
have a mortgage. The income levels of those in each tenure type are shown in
Table 2.13; in privately rented unfurnished accommodation and furnished tenancies
there is a disproportionate number of families at low income levels; the proportion
with high income levels is lowest in council housing. There is however a wide
distribution of income levels in all types of tenure.

The availability of five consumer durables (owned or hired) is shown in
Table 2.14. For all, availability increases with income level but the extent of
variation differs greatly. Even at the lowest income level, 92 per cent have a

television, compared to 98 per cent in the highest income level; by contrast
the availability of a car varied from 27 per cent to 87 per cent of families
between income levels.   Thus ownership or access to consumer durables is
clearly related to income - but the relationship is far from simple.

The analysis in this study is almost entirely based on incomes in relation
to SB levels.   This measure of income level depends crucially on the SB scales,
in particular on how those scales are related for families of different sizes
and with different ages of children.   The level of SB scales is, in this
regard, less important since the results are presented in a way which in most
cases allows comparisons to be made at, for example, SB level and 140 per cent
of SB level; it is open to the reader to choose which level is of most interest.
But having used the SB scales it is not, however, open to the reader to consider
the consequences of using a different relativity between families of different
sizes.   For example in all families the needs of a spouse are assessed on the
SB scale at about 60 per cent of the needs of the head.   There is no remedy for
this rigidity save to use throughout a multiplicity of different equivalence
scales, which is impossible for reasons of space.   Here a simple comparison is
made between the distribution analysed using the SB scales and using alternative
scales.   The results are shown in Table 2.15.   In the first column family
income is shown which takes no account at all of family size.   In the second
column income per adult equivalent is shown based on the SB scales.   In the
third column income per person is used which in effect treats all family members
including children as of equal weight.   It will be seen that the degree of
equality, as measured by the Gini coefficient or Atkinson measure, differ
considerably but that using the SB scale the measured inequality is lowest.
This does not of course prove the SB scales embody an appropriate equivalence
scale (which has been questioned, for example by Piachaud, 1979).   Rather the
differences serve as a warning that the results depend crucially on the

definition of "income level" that is used.

Finally in this chapter the distribution of incomes described here is compared with a similar analysis of the 1977 Family Expenditure Survey carried out by the Department of Health and Social Security. The latter analysis used either long-term or short-term SB levels depending on the level to which a family might have been eligible and is not therefore fully comparable. However a crude comparison is possible, as shown in Table 2.16; for this purpose the estimates in the analysis reported here have been grossed-up to give approximate estimates for Great Britain. It will be seen that the results presented here are broadly compatible and consistent with the results of the Government analysis of the Family Expenditure Survey.

TABLE 2.1

Income Levels by Type of Family

Percentages

Family Normal Income as % of SB Level*	Elderly Couple	Elderly Man	Elderly Woman	Couple, No child	Couple, 1 child	Couple, 2 ch'n.	Couple, 3 ch'n.	Couple, 4 ch'n.	Couple, 5+ ch'n.	Lone Parent 1+ ch'n.	Single Man	Single Woman	All Families	All Individuals
Under 80	2.2	7.8	10.7	2.2	2.5	2.9	2.5	9.0	6.4	20.0	8.7	12.7	6.4	5.1
80-	6.0	11.1	15.7	1.3	1.2	1.1	1.6	5.2	17.0	12.9	2.5	4.0	4.7	3.7
100-	30.8	32.6	42.5	2.8	4.5	5.7	7.9	11.9	10.6	14.6	5.1	8.5	12.9	10.4
120-	17.8	17.0	10.3	3.9	6.6	7.3	12.0	11.9	10.6	10.8	5.4	10.6	8.5	8.6
140-	26.7	18.1	12.4	17.3	29.5	36.1	41.0	42.5	40.4	25.8	24.7	31.1	25.3	28.8
200-	11.1	7.4	5.2	36.0	40.9	36.7	23.8	15.7	12.8	11.9	33.3	23.2	26.5	28.5
300-	4.1	4.8	2.5	33.1	13.1	8.8	9.3	3.7	2.1	3.1	18.1	8.8	13.9	13.2
500+	1.2	1.1	0.7	3.4	1.7	1.5	1.9	-	-	1.0	2.2	1.1	1.8	1.8
All	100	100	100	100	100	100	100	100	100	100	100	100	100	100
N	730	270	1083	1799	908	1072	366	134	47	295	1378	1070	9152	19697

TABLE 2.2

Distribution of families by type of family and income level

Percentages

| Type of family | Under 90 | Family normal income as % of SB level | | | | | | | All incomes |
		90-	100-	120-	140-	200-	300-	500+	
Elderly couple	2.7	10.3	19.1	16.7	8.4	3.3	2.4	5.5	8.0
Elderly man	3.6	7.0	7.5	5.9	2.1	0.8	1.0	1.8	3.0
Elderly woman	19.8	39.8	39.0	14.4	5.8	2.3	2.1	4.8	11.8
Couple, no children	6.7	5.6	4.2	9.0	13.4	26.7	46.9	37.0	19.7
Couple, 1 child	3.9	2.6	3.5	7.7	11.6	15.3	9.4	9.1	9.9
Couple, 2 children	5.3	2.8	5.2	10.0	16.7	16.2	7.4	9.7	11.7
Couple, 3 children	1.5	1.4	2.5	5.6	6.5	3.6	2.7	4.2	4.0
Couple, 4 children	2.1	1.6	1.4	2.1	2.5	0.9	0.4	-	1.5
Couple, 5+ children	0.5	1.9	0.4	0.6	0.8	0.2	0.1	-	0.5
Lone parent, 1+ child	10.1	8.9	3.6	4.1	3.3	1.4	0.7	1.8	3.2
Single man	20.5	8.0	5.9	9.5	14.7	18.9	19.6	18.8	15.1
Single woman	23.2	10.1	7.7	14.5	14.4	10.2	7.4	7.3	11.7
TOTAL	100	100	100	100	100	100	100	100	100

TABLE 2.3

Distribution of individuals by type of family and income level

Percentages

Type of family	Family normal income as % of SB level								Proportion of all individuals
	Under 90	90-	100-	120-	140-	200-	300-	500+	
Elderly couple	3.2	12.1	22.0	15.5	6.9	2.9	2.3	5.2	7.5
Elderly man	2.2	4.1	4.3	2.7	0.9	0.4	0.5	0.9	1.4
Elderly woman	12.0	23.3	22.5	6.6	2.4	1.0	1.0	2.3	5.5
Couple, no children	7.8	6.5	4.9	8.3	11.0	23.1	45.9	35.3	18.3
Couple, 1 child	6.9	4.5	6.0	10.6	14.2	19.8	13.7	13.0	13.8
Couple, 2 children	12.5	6.5	11.9	18.4	27.3	28.0	14.5	18.5	21.8
Couple, 3 children	4.5	4.1	7.1	13.0	13.2	7.7	6.5	10.1	9.3
Couple, 4 children	7.2	5.7	4.7	5.7	6.0	2.2	1.2	-	4.1
Couple, 5+ children	2.4	8.8	1.8	2.2	2.5	0.8	0.3	-	1.8
Lone parent, 1+ child	15.5	13.9	6.9	5.8	3.7	1.5	0.9	2.3	4.2
Single man	12.1	4.6	3.4	4.4	6.0	8.2	9.6	9.0	7.0
Single woman	13.7	5.9	4.4	6.7	5.9	4.4	3.6	3.5	5.4
All individuals	100	100	100	100	100	100	100	100	100

TABLE 2.4

Families in multi-family households

	Proportion in multi-family households	Mean implicit transfer within households
Type of family	%	pence per week
Elderly couple	14.9	+ 67
Elderly man	34.4	+ 168
Elderly woman	33.4	+ 240
Couple, no children	27.6	- 206
Couple, 1 child	26.8	- 140
Couple, 2 children	14.1	- 70
Couple, 3 children	13.1	- 20
Couple, 4 children	19.4	+ 20
Couple, 5+ children	12.8	- 51
Lone parent, 1+ child	39.3	+ 122
Single man	80.1	+ 26
Single woman	76.5	+ 378
Total	39.0	-
Family normal income as % of SB level		
Under 90	50.8	+ 670
90-	45.4	+ 456
100-	29.9	+ 247
120-	37.4	+ 299
140-	40.3	+ 158
200-	40.3	- 148
300-	37.5	- 520
500-	29.7	-1266
Total	39.0	-

TABLE 2.5

Household income levels by type of family

Percentages

Household Income as % of SB level	Type of Family												
	Elderly Couple	Elderly Man	Elderly Woman	Couple, no child	Couple, 1 child	Couple, 2 ch'n.	Couple, 3 ch'n.	Couple, 4 ch'n.	Couple, 5+ ch'n.	Lone Parent, 1+ child	Single Man	Single Woman	TOTAL
Under 80	2.2	6.7	9.0	2.1	2.1	3.0	2.7	10.4	6.4	14.2	3.9	5.0	4.3
90-	5.6	7.0	9.1	0.9	1.1	0.7	1.4	3.7	17.0	10.2	1.5	2.1	3.1
100-	29.0	31.5	35.5	2.7	4.0	5.4	6.6	11.2	10.6	14.2	3.7	6.4	11.2
120-	15.5	13.3	9.4	3.9	7.3	6.7	13.9	9.0	12.8	14.9	6.5	9.4	8.3
140-	29.7	22.2	22.0	18.7	31.9	39.2	40.7	46.3	40.4	28.8	28.1	32.0	28.5
200-	12.5	11.5	11.3	39.4	40.4	35.2	23.8	16.4	10.6	14.6	39.9	33.1	30.1
300-	4.2	6.7	3.2	29.6	11.9	8.5	9.6	3.0	2.1	2.0	14.4	10.8	12.9
500+	1.2	1.1	0.6	2.7	1.3	1.3	1.4	-	-	1.0	2.0	1.2	1.5
All	100	100	100	100	100	100	100	100	100	100	100	100	100

-20-

TABLE 2.6

Current and normal income levels of families

Percentages

Family current income as % of SB level	Family normal income as % of SB level								
	Under 90	90-	100-	120-	140-	200-	300-	500+	All
Under 90	98.3	0.7	1.4	2.3	1.9	1.8	2.6	1.8	8.0
90-	0.7	97.7	0.6	0.8	0.6	0.2	0.2	0.6	5.0
100-	0.3	0.7	92.8	3.7	1.1	0.6	0.4	0.6	12.8
120-	0.3	0.9	3.8	84.1	2.9	0.4	0.4	0.6	8.6
140-	0.3	-	1.3	8.2	84.7	6.6	1.5	2.4	24.3
200-	-	-	0.1	0.8	8.6	84.2	9.9	3.0	26.0
300-	-	-	0.1	0.1	0.3	6.1	83.2	6.7	13.4
500-	-	-	-	-	-	0.2	1.8	84.2	1.8
ALL	100	100	100	100	100	100	100	100	100
ALL	6.4	4.7	12.9	8.5	25.3	26.5	13.9	1.8	100
N	585	427	1179	780	2320	2425	1271	165	9152

TABLE 2.7

Distribution of incomes and income levels

	Net income (£ per week)			Income relative to SB level		
	Family normal income	Family current income	Household normal income	Family normal income	Family current income	Household normal income
Proportion below:						
SB level				11.1%	13.0%	7.4%
140% of SB level				32.5%	34.4%	26.9%
5th percentile	17.11	16.10	22.74	0.86	0.78	0.93
Lowest decile	20.61	19.82	28.00	0.98	0.94	1.04
Lower Quartile	29.85	29.05	48.08	1.22	1.18	1.35
Median	50.38	49.21	77.33	1.81	1.78	1.87
Upper quartile	79.06	77.63	109.14	2.57	2.53	2.53
Highest decile	104.78	104.57	144.43	3.36	3.36	3.28
95th percentile	125.11	125.22	171.29	3.93	3.96	3.86
Gini coefficient	.339	.346	.311	.280	.292	.255
Atkinson measure						
$\alpha = -0.5$	.7459	.6863	.7642	.8272	.8281	.8488
$\alpha = -1.0$	.6434	.2024	.6900	.7453	.7183	.7977
$\alpha = -2.0$	.2312	.0051	.5612	.3539	.2771	.6486

TABLE 2.8

Characteristics by age - Men

Percentages

					Age							All ages
	16-	18-	21-	25-	35-	45-	55-	60-	65-	70-	75+	
Type of family												
Lone adult	100.0	91.4	54.9	17.2	10.1	11.2	12.0	13.1	20.3	24.7	37.6	24.5
Lone adult + child(ren)	-	-	0.2	0.2	1.2	1.0	0.8	0.4	-	-	-	0.5
Couple, no children	-	3.1	26.1	20.0	10.3	40.7	72.1	80.8	79.5	75.3	62.4	37.5
Couple + child(ren)	-	5.5	18.8	62.6	78.4	47.1	15.0	5.7	0.2	-	-	37.5
Family income level (as % of SB level)												
Under 100	20.8	10.0	6.9	4.9	4.5	4.3	4.2	9.1	8.6	12.0	13.4	6.7
100-	39.6	11.3	7.0	11.3	10.4	7.9	6.8	11.4	41.5	51.5	53.4	16.5
140-	31.2	44.7	19.8	28.9	28.3	22.8	22.7	24.9	26.1	22.9	22.4	26.6
200-	7.1	28.0	44.5	31.2	37.1	38.6	36.9	34.6	15.8	8.7	6.2	31.1
300+	1.3	5.0	21.7	23.7	19.7	26.4	29.3	20.1	8.0	4.8	4.5	19.1
Mean income level	1.33	1.83	2.34	2.34	2.33	2.55	2.61	2.30	1.69	1.59	1.47	2.22
Economic status												
Working as employee	85.1	84.4	84.8	85.2	80.9	83.9	82.9	70.5	14.7	9.0	2.4	70.8
Self-employed	1.3	0.8	4.5	8.4	11.7	9.2	7.0	5.7	4.8	4.5	0.7	7.2
Unemployed	13.0	9.7	6.9	4.5	4.3	2.9	3.2	4.2	-	-	-	4.0
Sick or disabled	-	0.9	0.6	0.3	2.7	3.5	5.6	12.4	0.2	-	-	2.5
Retired	-	-	-	-	-	-	0.8	6.3	79.5	85.2	96.2	14.3
Unoccupied	0.6	4.2	3.2	1.6	0.5	0.6	0.4	0.8	0.9	1.2	0.7	1.2
N = 100%	154	360	494	1480	1123	1070	498	474	463	332	290	6738

TABLE 2.9

Characteristics by age – Women

Percentages

	Age											All ages
	16-	18-	21-	25-	35-	45-	55-	60-	65-	70-	75-	
Type of family												
Lone adult	95.1	68.2	28.9	7.9	7.2	13.7	23.7	34.6	40.7	57.5	80.2	28.8
Lone adult + child(ren)	1.2	4.0	5.4	5.3	8.0	2.9	1.7	0.3	-	-	-	3.5
Couple, no children	1.9	14.5	34.6	14.7	11.5	50.3	68.9	64.4	59.2	42.4	19.8	23.9
Couple + child(ren)	1.9	13.3	31.2	72.1	73.3	33.3	5.7	0.7	-	-	-	33.9
Family income level (as % of SB level)												
Under 100	27.2	19.1	9.7	6.5	6.6	3.9	8.6	10.5	13.8	16.7	29.8	10.7
100-	42.0	19.1	10.5	13.3	10.9	9.8	12.9	33.3	49.2	54.6	52.0	22.4
140-	24.7	39.6	30.5	30.5	30.7	20.9	22.7	26.0	21.3	17.5	12.3	25.7
200-	3.7	15.9	29.9	31.4	35.5	38.8	34.0	17.8	10.7	7.8	4.0	25.9
300+	2.5	6.4	19.3	18.2	16.4	26.6	21.9	12.5	5.0	3.4	2.0	15.2
Mean income level	1.27	1.64	2.15	2.20	2.22	2.55	2.34	1.83	1.50	1.45	1.24	2.02
Economic status												
Working as employee	80.2	70.8	65.6	50.7	64.9	66.1	54.1	25.5	8.0	4.4	0.5	46.6
Self-employed	0.6	1.4	6.5	9.1	6.5	4.4	3.6	2.7	3.0	2.4	0.4	4.9
Unemployed	13.6	9.2	4.1	1.2	2.0	0.8	1.0	0.2	-	-	-	1.8
Sick or disabled	-	0.3	0.2	0.3	1.3	2.2	2.7	1.0	0.2	-	-	0.9
Retired	-	-	-	-	-	0.1	2.4	27.2	38.7	38.3	31.5	9.6
Unoccupied	5.6	18.2	23.7	38.7	25.3	26.4	36.1	43.3	50.1	54.9	67.6	36.2
N = 100%	162	346	558	1496	1125	1098	582	584	535	412	571	7469

TABLE 2.10

Multi-family households and income levels by age - men

Percentage:

Age	Proportion in multi-family households	Proportion below SB level		Proportion below 140% of SB level	
		Based on family income	Based on household income	Based on family income	Based on household income
Under 18	99.4	20.8	2.6	60.4	20.1
18-	90.6	10.0	5.0	21.4	17.5
21-	54.0	6.9	4.5	14.0	12.6
25-	16.0	4.9	4.3	16.3	15.2
35-	24.6	4.5	4.2	14.8	14.4
45-	46.2	4.3	3.1	12.2	12.3
55-	39.0	4.2	3.4	11.0	11.6
60-	26.8	9.1	7.0	20.5	19.2
65-	20.7	8.6	8.4	50.1	44.9
70-	19.3	12.0	9.0	63.5	57.2
75 and over	20.3	13.4	11.0	66.8	60.0
All ages	34.0	6.7	5.0	23.2	20.7

TABLE 2.11

Multi-family households and income levels by age - women

Percentages

Age	Proportion in multi-family households	Proportion below SB level		Proportion below 140% of SB level	
		Based on family income	Based on household income	Based on family income	Based on household income
Under 18	93.8	27.2	8.7	69.2	26.6
18-	71.7	19.1	9.2	38.2	23.9
21-	31.2	9.7	6.8	20.2	17.2
25-	10.3	6.5	5.5	18.8	18.8
35-	33.3	6.6	5.1	17.5	17.5
45-	47.3	3.9	2.7	13.7	12.9
55-	34.2	8.6	6.4	21.5	18.1
60-	27.2	10.5	7.7	43.8	37.3
65-	21.7	13.8	11.4	63.0	56.1
70-	21.6	16.7	13.4	71.3	62.2
75 and over	30.5	29.8	19.8	81.8	64.5
All ages	39.0	11.1	7.4	32.5	26.9

TABLE 2.12

Housing tenure by type of family and income level

Percentages

	Owned outright	Owned with mortgage	Council rented unfurnished	Other rented unfurnished	Rented furnished	Rent free	All tenures
Type of family							
Elderly couple	48.5	3.4	33.3	11.6	0.3	2.9	100
Elderly man	41.5	3.3	36.3	15.9	0.4	2.6	100
Elderly woman	34.8	6.3	39.7	16.3	0.8	2.0	100
Couple, no children	19.5	34.6	32.7	8.3	2.4	2.3	100
Couple, 1 child	9.7	47.8	32.5	5.9	2.5	1.5	100
Couple, 2 children	6.9	57.9	26.5	5.2	1.6	1.9	100
Couple, 3 children	6.0	52.2	34.4	4.6	0.3	2.5	100
Couple, 4 children	11.2	34.3	47.0	3.7	0.7	3.0	100
Couple, 5+ children	17.0	34.0	36.2	8.5	-	4.3	100
Lone parent, 1+ child	8.8	19.3	59.7	10.2	1.4	0.7	100
Single man	16.6	24.5	41.3	9.1	6.6	1.9	100
Single woman	19.6	22.3	40.7	8.8	6.5	2.1	100
Family normal income as % of SB level							
Under 90	14.9	14.5	50.4	11.8	7.4	1.0	100
90-	24.4	11.2	47.5	13.6	1.4	1.9	100
100-	24.3	9.2	48.9	14.2	1.4	1.9	100
120-	23.8	16.5	44.1	11.0	2.1	2.4	100
140-	18.9	28.8	38.3	8.5	2.8	2.7	100
200-	18.2	38.1	31.4	7.4	3.1	1.9	100
300-	21.1	49.2	19.7	5.7	2.8	1.7	100
500-	32.7	47.3	4.8	6.7	4.2	4.2	100
All families	20.4	29.1	36.3	9.2	2.9	2.1	100

TABLE 2.13

Distribution of families by income level and housing tenure

Percentages

Family normal income as % of SB level	Owned outright	Owned with mortgage	Council rented unfurnished	Other rented unfurnished	Rented furnished	Rent free	All tenures
Under 90	4.7	3.2	8.9	8.2	16.3	3.1	6.4
90-	5.6	1.8	6.1	6.9	2.3	4.2	4.7
100-	15.4	4.1	17.3	20.0	6.5	11.5	12.9
120-	10.0	4.8	10.3	10.2	6.1	9.9	8.5
140-	23.5	25.0	26.7	23.5	24.7	33.0	25.3
200-	23.6	34.7	22.9	21.3	28.1	23.6	26.5
300-	14.4	23.4	7.5	8.6	13.3	11.0	13.9
500-	2.9	2.9	0.2	1.3	2.7	3.7	1.8
Total	100	100	100	100	100	100	100
N	1866	2666	3325	841	263	191	9152

TABLE 2.14

Consumer durables by type of family and income level

Percentages

	Proportion of families in households with:				
	Television	Refrigerator	Washing machine	Telephone	Car
Type of family					
Elderly couple	97.7	86.6	71.0	52.9	41.1
Elderly man	91.9	70.4	44.8	34.8	30.7
Elderly woman	92.6	78.6	50.4	46.4	20.4
Couple, no children	97.6	96.1	83.2	64.4	74.0
Couple, 1 child	99.2	95.6	88.9	63.2	75.0
Couple, 2 children	99.0	97.5	92.8	66.4	78.8
Couple, 3 children	97.8	97.3	94.0	63.7	75.1
Couple, 4 children	96.3	93.3	88.8	56.7	60.4
Couple, 5+ children	93.6	91.5	80.9	48.9	68.1
Lone parent, 1+ child	97.6	86.1	75.9	44.7	32.9
Single man	94.8	87.8	69.8	50.7	62.2
Single woman	95.1	91.0	69.7	59.2	51.7
Total	96.4	90.4	75.6	57.1	58.5
Family normal income as % of SB level					
Under 90	92.0	81.0	61.0	40.2	37.6
90-	93.2	81.3	61.4	41.9	33.3
100-	94.1	77.7	60.9	36.1	27.0
120-	96.8	88.2	73.3	45.8	46.7
140-	97.8	93.2	81.0	56.3	60.5
200-	97.9	94.7	81.4	65.0	70.8
300-	96.1	96.8	80.9	77.6	82.6
500-	97.6	97.6	77.0	94.5	86.7
Total	96.4	90.4	75.6	57.1	58.5

TABLE 2.15

Inequality of income by measure of income

	Family income (net income less housing costs)	Income per adult equivalent	Income per person
Gini coefficient	.344	.280	.302
Atkinson measure			
$\alpha = -0.5$	.7337	.8272	.8035
$\alpha = -1.0$	.6278	.7453	.7205
$\alpha = -2.0$	.2437	.3539	.3813

TABLE 2.16

Comparison of studies of income distribution

Number of individuals (in thousands)

	FES-present analysis 1977		FES-DHSS analysis[a] December 1977
	Less than 100% of long-term SB level	Less than 120% of long-term SB level	Less than 120% of long/short term SB level
Elderly couple	343	2368	1860
Elderly single person	969	2971	2740
Couple, no children	357	1038	410
Couples with children	1566	5791	2890
Single persons with children	726	1407	1190
Single persons without children	944	1930	960
ALL	4905	15505	10070

Source: a. Table 47.07, Social Security Statistics, 1980.

Chapter 3

Income Distribution and the Labour Market

The greater part of incomes is derived from paid employment. A person's ability or decision to participate in the labour market is one of the most important determinants of income distribution. For those in paid work, hourly earnings are crucial in determining income from employment. In Part A of this chapter economic status is considered and in Part B hourly earnings are analysed.

A. Economic status

The population may be divided into the economically active - those in full-time and part-time paid employment, the self-employed and employers, and those without employment but actively seeking work - and the economically inactive - those out of the labour force due to disability, retirement, or who are classified as unoccupied.

The economic status of heads of families and their spouses is shown, by type of family, in Tables 3.1 and 3.2. The broad picture is relatively clear: most of the elderly are inactive and most non-elderly heads are active; only among lone parents and spouses are there similar proportions of active and inactive. This broad picture conceals important features; for example, the unemployment of the head and economic activity of the spouse vary with the number of children; the balance between full-time and part-time work is very different for heads and spouses. While the proportion of spouses defined as unemployed is much higher for heads than for spouses, if the unoccupied are included the position is altogether reversed.

The analysis by type of family distinguishes only by number of children. The importance of the age of the children for mother's employment is analysed in Table 3.3. It will be seen that much greater differences exist between mothers' economic activity when distinguished by age of youngest child than existed by number of children (Table 3.2). Only 2.5 per cent of mothers with a child under 2 were in full-time work and nearly two-thirds were economically inactive; by contrast, where the youngest child was aged 11 or over only one-fifth were economically inactive.

The relationship of income levels to the heads' economic status is considered in Table 3.4.   Of those in full-time work, 1.2 per cent were below SB level compared with over half the unemployed, over one-quarter of the disabled and 16.8 per cent of the retired.   The importance of economic status is thus clear.

B.   Hourly earnings

The distribution of earnings is considered here in relation to hourly earnings.   Most people are paid on an hourly basis and any policies designed to alter the distribution of earnings would almost inevitably have to be based on hourly rates of pay.   The distribution of hourly earnings is shown in Table 3.5.   This table is divided by sex because of the very great differences in the distribution of men's and women's earnings and also divided on the basis of age because of the substantial difference that exists between the earnings of young and older workers.   There are of course differences between all age groups but those between the young worker, often on an apprenticeship or training scheme, and adult workers is the most marked.   It will be seen from Table 3.5 that 5.7 per cent of adult men earned less than 100 pence per hour but 37.7 per cent of adult women, over half of young men and over two-thirds of young women did so.   At the other end of the earnings range, 60.5 per cent of adult men earned over 150 pence per hour whereas only 19.5 per cent of adult women did so.

Hourly earnings of family heads in relation to income level are shown in Tables 3.6, 3.7 and 3.8.   Of those under SB level, over one-third had hourly earnings of under 50 pence and two-thirds had hourly earnings of under 75 pence. By contrast only 6.7 per cent of all family heads had hourly earnings of under 75 pence (Table 3.6).   A slightly different perspective is given by Table 3.7: of those earning under 50 pence per hour over half were above SB level and of those earning 50-75 pence per hour 90 per cent were above SB level.   Of families which recorded hourly earnings, 4.7 per cent had both hourly earnings of the head of less than 75 pence and an income below 140 per cent of SB level (Table 3.8).

Thus, those with the lowest hourly earnings are more likely to have a low income level. But there are considerable proportions of those with low income levels who had relatively high hourly earnings. There are also considerable proportions of those with low hourly earnings who have relatively high income levels. To understand why this is the case it is worth recalling that there are variations in hours worked per week, unearned income, family size, and housing cost - all of which affect the family's income level.

The extent of low hourly earnings of family heads in relation to sex, age, type of family and income level is summarised in Table 3.9. Great differences exist, as has been seen above, and this is reflected in the mean hourly earnings which are 50 per cent higher for men than for women, 92 per cent higher for those over 21 than for those under 21, 54 per cent higher for couples with children than for lone parents with children, and 233 per cent higher for those in the highest income group than the lowest income group.

The relationship between hourly earnings and income levels is explored in more detail for men in Tables 3.10 and 3.11 and for women in Tables 3.12 and 3.13. Whereas male family members included in the Family Expenditure Survey have been automatically assigned as family head, women may be either heads or spouses. The analysis in Tables 3.5 - 3.9 only includes women who are family heads. In Tables 3.12 and 3.13 all women, whether head or spouse, have been combined. Comparing men and women, fewer men at lower income levels have low hourly earnings (Tables 3.10 and 3.12) but,of those with low hourly earnings, more men than women are at low income levels. This pattern reflects both the lower earnings of women than men and the fact that many working women are in two-earner families.

The extent of low pay and low income levels varies by occupation and by industry. In Tables 3.14, 3.15 and 3.16 the extent of low pay is shown by occupation and by industry together with the extent of low income levels of workers in those sectors. In addition the extent to which low pay and low

income levels occur simultaneously is also shown. The analyses in these tables
are not based on families but rather on individual workers, although income
levels are, of course, still those of the family; a family with both a man
and a woman working will therefore be counted twice for the purposes of these
tables.

In relation to occupation it will be seen from Table 3.14 that the highest
incidence of low hourly earnings occurs among shop assistants and unskilled
manual workers both for men and for women. The greatest extent of low income
levels also arises in these two sectors and, consequently, the same is true
of men and women experiencing both hourly earnings and low income levels.

Comparing industries in Tables 3.15, the greatest extent of low pay among
men occurs in the agriculture, distributive and service sectors. There is a
substantial difference between the extent of low pay and the extent of low
income levels in all sectors but those sectors with more low pay have more men
who are both low paid and in low income level families. Among women, as shown
in Table 3.16, there is a far greater extent of low pay. But there is also a
bigger difference between the proportion who are low paid and the proportion
who are in low income families. For example in professional and scientific
industries 5 per cent of men and 28 per cent of women earned 100 pence per hour
or less; the proportion of men and women in that industry who were in families
at or below 140 per cent of SB level was, however, little different; on the
other hand a higher proportion of women than men were both low paid and low
income level. Comparing women who were heads of families with those who were
married (which is only possible because of sample numbers for certain industries)
there is little difference in the extent of low pay but a very great difference
in the extent of low family income levels.

Thus, there are occupations and industries where low pay and low income
levels are most common but it is not possible to identify occupations or
industries where there is a very great overlap between low pay and low income

levels.   It is not therefore possible to identify sectors where policies on low pay would be particularly effective in tackling low income levels.   A general policy to tackle low pay has therefore been considered, with results presented in Chapter 5.

TABLE 3.1

Economic status of head of family by type of family

Percentages

Economic status of head	Elderly couple	Elderly man	Elderly woman	Couple no ch'n	Couple 1 ch	Couple 2 ch'n	Couple 3 ch'n	Couple 4 ch'n	Couple 5+ ch'n	Lone parent 1+ ch'n	Single man	Single woman	All families
Employee	10.3	5.6	7.0	81.5	85.9	83.4	76.5	73.9	68.1	50.2	80.3	79.8	63.7
In full-time work	2.1	1.9	1.8	75.5	82.0	79.8	72.1	67.9	63.8	28.8	75.4	67.7	57.2
In part-time work	8.1	3.3	5.1	2.1	0.9	0.8	1.4	-	2.1	19.7	2.2	10.0	4.1
Self-employed or employer	3.0	4.4	1.6	6.3	8.8	11.3	16.4	10.4	6.4	5.4	3.7	2.0	5.8
Unemployed	-	-	-	2.6	3.5	3.7	4.6	11.9	17.0	4.4	7.8	7.1	3.9
Disabled, not seeking work	0.1	-	0.2	3.8	1.2	1.0	1.4	2.2	6.4	2.0	2.2	1.9	1.8
Retired	85.8	88.5	40.7	4.4	0.2	-	-	-	-	-	1.3	0.7	15.5
Unoccupied	0.8	1.5	50.5	0.8	0.1	0.2	0.3	0.7	-	37.3	3.8	8.0	9.0
All	100	100	100	100	100	100	100	100	100	100	100	100	100

Notes: The division of employees into full-time and part-time uses different variables so that they do not precisely sum to the total of employees.

The total - All - includes those sick or injured who are intending to seek work.

TABLE 3.2

Economic status of spouse by type of family

Percentages

Economic status of head	Elderly couple	Couple no children	Couple 1 child	Couple 2 children	Couple 3 children	Couple 4 children	Couple 5+ children	All couples
Employee								
In full-time work	9.7	61.4	48.8	48.6	56.8	45.5	40.4	48.0
In part-time work	2.7	36.1	15.6	10.8	10.7	13.4	19.1	19.7
	6.3	23.1	32.2	36.0	44.0	29.9	19.1	26.7
Self-employed or employer	2.2	3.6	8.5	11.5	5.7	9.0	2.1	6.2
Unemployed	0.1	1.4	0.9	0.7	1.1	0.7	-	0.9
Disabled, not seeking work	0.7	1.1	0.6	0.1	0.3	-	-	0.6
Retired	27.7	3.7	0.1	-	-	-	-	5.3
Unoccupied	59.6	28.5	41.1	39.1	36.1	44.8	57.4	38.7
All	100	100	100	100	100	100	100	100

See notes to Table 3.1

TABLE 3.3

Economic status of spouses by age of youngest child

Percentages

Economic status of head	Age of youngest child			
	Under 2	2-4	5-10	11 or over
Employee				
In full-time work	17.4	32.3	53.8	59.8
In part-time work	2.5	5.3	12.4	21.2
	13.8	26.5	39.7	36.6
Self-employed or employer	11.0	12.0	8.1	3.6
Unemployed	1.4	0.5	0.8	0.5
Disabled, not seeking work	-	0.3	-	0.7
Retired	-	-	-	0.1
Unoccupied	62.8	46.2	27.2	20.2
All	100	100	100	100
N	516	600	951	768

See notes to Table 3.1

TABLE 3.4

Income levels by economic status of head of family

Percentages

Economic status of head	Family normal income as % of SB level								TOTAL	All families	N
	Under 90	90-	100-	120-	140-	200-	300-	500-			
Employee											
In full-time work	0.9	0.9	4.0	6.7	30.5	36.3	18.9	1.8	100	63.7	5827
In part-time work	0.5	0.7	3.4	6.4	30.8	37.5	19.0	1.7	100	57.2	5232
	5.5	3.2	11.9	12.9	32.5	18.7	13.2	2.1	100	4.1	379
Self-employed or employer	13.7	3.8	8.9	8.1	19.6	22.0	16.4	7.5	100	5.8	531
Unemployed	44.7	9.8	8.7	5.1	13.2	11.0	6.2	1.4	100	3.9	356
Disabled, not seeking work	12.4	16.8	22.4	13.0	25.5	8.7	1.2	-	100	1.8	161
Retired	6.5	10.3	35.8	15.4	19.9	8.1	3.3	0.8	100	15.5	1414
Unoccupied	21.6	17.1	38.3	10.3	7.9	3.0	1.1	0.7	100	9.0	825
All	6.4	4.7	12.9	8.5	25.3	26.5	13.9	1.8	100	100	9152

See notes to Table 3.1

TABLE 3.5

Distribution of hourly earnings

Percentages

Hourly earnings (pence)	Men		Women	
	Under 21	21 and over	Under 21	21 and over
Under 50	5.5	0.3	8.2	2.5
50-	22.5	1.0	32.2	8.8
75-	27.6	4.4	31.7	26.4
100-	24.3	14.1	19.8	28.0
125-	12.6	19.8	5.7	14.8
150-	6.2	32.6	2.3	10.8
200 and over	1.3	27.9	-	8.7
All	100	100	100	100
N	453	4391	388	3123

TABLE 3.6

Hourly earnings of heads by income level

Percentages

| | Family normal income as percentage of SB level | | | | | |
	Under 100	100-	140-	200-	300+	All
Hourly earnings (pence)						
Under 50	36.9	5.7	0.5	0.1	-	1.4
50-	29.1	27.7	4.6	1.0	0.3	5.3
75-	17.5	17.8	18.5	5.1	1.2	10.0
100-	5.8	19.8	24.5	15.7	5.6	16.6
125-	6.8	15.6	19.2	22.7	10.4	18.0
150-	1.0	11.2	22.5	32.4	32.0	26.5
200 and over	2.9	2.2	10.2	23.0	50.4	22.2
All earnings	100	100	100	100	100	100
N	103	635	1803	2149	1228	5918

TABLE 3.7

Income level by hourly earnings of head

Percentages

Family normal income as percentage of SB level	Hourly earnings of head (pence)							All hourly earnings
	Under 50	50-	75-	100-	125-	150-	200+	
Under 100	44.7	9.6	3.1	0.6	0.7	-	0.2	1.7
100-	42.4	56.1	19.2	12.9	9.3	4.5	1.1	10.7
140-	10.6	26.4	56.7	45.0	32.4	25.9	14.0	30.5
200-	2.4	6.7	18.5	34.5	45.6	44.5	37.6	36.3
300+	-	1.3	2.5	7.0	12.0	25.1	47.1	20.8
All income levels	100	100	100	100	100	100	100	100
N	85	314	589	980	1067	1568	1315	5918

TABLE 3.8

Income levels and hourly earnings

Percentages

	Hourly earnings of head (pence)				
	Under 75	75-	100-	150-	All
Family normal income as percentage of SB level					
Under 140	4.7	2.2	4.0	1.5	12.4
140-	1.6	5.6	13.3	10.0	30.5
200+	0.5	2.1	17.3	37.2	57.1
All	6.7	10.0	34.6	48.7	100.0

TABLE 3.9

Head's hourly earnings

	Proportion of families with head's hourly earnings (%)		Mean Hourly Earnings Pence
	Under 75p	Under 100p	
Head of family:			
Male	3.8	10.4	174
Female	19.9	45.1	116
Under 21	34.6	64.1	91
21 or over	2.5	9.4	175
Type of family:			
Elderly	22.9	51.8	112
Couple, no children	0.5	3.7	177
Couple with child(ren)	0.8	3.5	195
Lone parent with child(ren)	9.9	35.6	127
Single person	16.0	35.8	128
Family normal income as % of SB level:			
Under 100	66.0	83.5	69
100-	33.4	51.2	102
140-	5.1	23.6	136
200-	1.1	6.2	171
300 and over	0.3	1.5	230
All families	6.8	16.8	163

TABLE 3.10

Hourly earnings of men by income level

Percentages

	Family normal income by percentage of SB level					
	Under 100	100-	140-	200-	300+	All
Hourly earnings (pence)						
Under 50	32.6	4.0	0.4	0.1	-	0.8
50-	18.6	17.9	3.2	0.8	0.3	3.0
75-	20.9	11.8	12.5	3.9	1.0	6.6
100-	7.0	23.6	21.4	14.3	5.1	15.0
125-	14.0	22.9	21.4	21.7	10.6	19.1
150-	2.3	16.5	28.2	33.6	32.9	30.1
200 and over	4.7	3.3	12.8	25.7	50.1	25.4
All earnings	100	100	100	100	100	100
N	43	424	1403	1866	1108	4844

TABLE 3.11

Hourly earnings of men by income level

Percentages

| Hourly earnings (pence) | Family normal income as percentage of SB level | | | | | | |
	Under 100	100-	140-	200-	300+	All	N
Under 50	35.9	43.6	15.4	5.1	-	100	39
50-	5.5	52.1	30.8	9.6	2.1	100	146
75-	2.8	15.7	55.3	22.6	3.5	100	318
100-	0.4	13.8	41.3	36.7	7.8	100	727
125-	0.6	10.5	32.4	43.7	12.7	100	926
150-	0.1	4.8	27.2	43.0	25.0	100	1458
200 and over	0.2	1.1	14.6	38.9	45.1	100	1230
All earnings	0.9	8.8	29.0	38.5	22.9	100	4844
N							

TABLE 3.12

Hourly earnings of women by income level

Percentages

	Family normal income as percentage of SB level					
	Under 100	100-	140-	200-	300+	All
Hourly earnings (pence)						
Under 50	28.7	8.0	3.7	1.4	0.9	3.1
50-	28.7	40.8	13.6	7.7	2.2	11.4
75-	21.8	31.2	37.6	28.6	12.4	27.0
100-	11.5	16.4	31.0	31.4	21.6	27.1
125-	4.6	1.6	9.3	18.1	17.2	13.8
150-	2.3	1.3	2.7	9.2	22.3	9.9
200 and over	2.3	0.6	2.1	3.5	23.3	7.7
All Earnings	100	100	100	100	100	100
N	87	311	918	1331	864	3511

TABLE 3.13

Hourly earnings of women by income level

Percentages

	Family normal income as percentage of SB level						
	Under 100	100-	140-	200-	300+	All	N
Hourly earnings (pence)							
Under 50	22.7	22.7	30.9	16.4	7.3	100	110
50-	6.3	31.8	31.3	25.8	4.8	100	399
75-	2.0	10.2	36.4	40.1	11.3	100	949
100-	1.1	5.4	30.0	44.0	19.7	100	951
125-	0.8	1.0	17.6	49.8	30.8	100	484
150-	0.6	1.2	7.2	35.4	55.6	100	347
200 and over	0.7	0.7	7.0	17.3	74.2	100	271
All Earnings	2.5	8.9	26.1	37.9	24.6	100	3511

TABLE 3.14

Earnings and income level by occupation

Percentages

Occupation		Hourly earnings 100p or less	Family normal income 140% of SB or less	Hourly earnings ≤ 100p and family normal income ≤ 140% of SB	N
Professional and technical	Men	3.0	2.8	0.8	507
	Women	14.6	2.8	1.4	288
	All	7.2	2.8	1.0	795
Administrative and managerial	Men	6.1	4.8	0.9	537
	Women	25.5	2.7	1.8	110
	All	9.4	4.4	1.1	647
Teachers	Men	0.7	2.1	-	143
	Women	2.0	-	-	201
	All	1.5	0.9	-	344
Clerical workers	Men	10.1	9.8	3.3	396
	Women	30.3	9.7	8.0	1093
	All	24.9	9.7	6.8	1489
Shop assistants	Men	43.2	18.2	15.9	44
	Women	84.3	16.9	16.1	255
	All	78.3	17.1	16.1	299
Skilled manual	Men	8.7	9.9	3.4	1936
	Women	51.4	13.0	12.6	247
	All	13.5	10.3	4.4	2183
Semi-skilled manual	Men	17.1	14.8	6.8	975
	Women	54.8	13.3	11.1	955
	All	35.8	14.1	8.9	1930
Unskilled manual	Men	26.4	13.2	5.8	258
	Women	68.8	22.0	17.3	359
	All	51.0	18.3	12.5	617

TABLE 3.15

Earnings and income level of men by industry

Percentages

SIC Order	Industry	Hourly earnings 100p or less	Family normal income 140% of SB or less	Hourly earnings ≤ 100p and family normal income ≤ 140% of SB	N
1.	Agriculture	28.3	16.2	6.1	99
2.	Mining	2.6	5.1	0.9	117
3.	Food, drink, tobacco	12.4	13.0	5.0	161
4.	Coal & petroleum	4.8*	-*	-*	21
5.	Chemical & allied	3.6	4.5	0.9	110
6.	Metal manufacture	3.0	4.1	1.8	169
7.	Mechanical eng.	10.9	8.3	3.6	302
8.	Instrument eng.	12.8*	7.7*	2.6*	39
9.	Electrical eng.	4.3	7.6	2.7	184
10.	Shipbuilding	8.9	5.4	-	56
11.	Vehicles	7.1	10.3	2.8	281
12.	Metal goods n.e.s.	15.7	13.6	7.1	140
13.	Textiles	15.0	8.0	2.0	100
14.	Leather, etc	-*	-*	-*	9
15.	Clothing & footwear	12.0*	16.0*	-*	25
16.	Bricks, pottery, etc.	11.3	24.5	5.7	53
17.	Timber furniture	14.3	7.8	2.6	77
18.	Paper printing	5.3	5.9	3.3	152
19.	Other manufacturing	10.8	12.2	5.4	74
20.	Construction	11.1	11.3	4.1	461
21.	Gas, electricity, water	1.8	6.4	0.9	109
22a.	Rail transport	4.2	9.5	3.2	95
22b.	Other transport	6.7	10.1	2.7	375
23.	Distributive trades	20.3	14.0	7.7	413
24.	Insurance, banking	7.7	6.1	2.0	196
25.	Professional, scientific	4.7	5.9	1.4	358
26a.	Miscellaneous services[a]	25.2	13.4	6.7	119
26b.	Miscellaneous services[b]	40.3	18.8	14.1	149
27a.	Armed forces	6.0	14.0	2.0	50
27b.	National government	5.7	3.8	0.6	157
27c.	Police & fire	-	4.7	-	64
27d.	Local Gov't.(excl.27c)	7.0	10.1	1.6	129

Note: * indicates a base of less than 50.

a. Laundries, cleaning, motor repairs, filling station, shoe repairs
b. Other miscellaneous services.

TABLE 3.16

Earnings and income level of women by industry

Percentages

SIC Order	Industry	Hourly earnings 100p or less	Family normal income 140% of SB or less	Hourly earnings ≤ 100p and family normal income ≤ 140% of SB	N
3.	Food, drink, tobacco	35.3	7.8	2.9	102
5.	Chemical & allied	14.8	3.7	1.9	54
7.	Mechanical eng.	38.2	5.5	1.8	55
9.	Electrical eng.	32.1	11.9	10.1	109
11.	Vehicles	18.3	6.7	5.0	60
12.	Metal goods n.e.s.	32.2	10.2	8.5	59
13.	Textiles	55.8	7.8	6.5	77
15.	Clothing and footwear	68.7	14.5	13.7	131
18.	Paper, printing	24.4	9.8	8.5	82
22b.	Transport & Comm (excl. Rail)	30.7	8.9	5.9	101
23.	Distributive Trades Heads	75.7	36.7	34.9	169
	Spouses	66.3	5.5	4.1	344
	All	69.4	15.8	14.2	513
24.	Insurance, banking etc. Heads	35.9	20.5	20.5	78
	Spouses	31.0	4.1	1.4	145
	All	32.7	9.9	8.1	223
25.	Professional, scientific Heads	25.9	10.4	8.1	259
	Spouses	28.5	2.6	1.4	666
	All	27.8	4.8	3.2	925
26a.	Miscellaneous services[a]	60.8	18.9	17.6	74
26b.	Miscellaneous services[b] Heads	67.9	53.7	47.8	134
	Spouses	72.2	14.3	13.5	342
	All	71.0	25.4	23.1	476
27c.	National government	15.3	-	-	118
27d.	Local gov't.	12.2	6.1	1.2	82

Note: Industries where less than 50 women in sample are omitted.

a. Laundries, cleaning, motor repairs, filling stations, shoe repairs
b. Other miscellaneous services.

Chapter 4

Income Distribution and Social Security

Social security is now by a substantial margin the largest category of public expenditure. It is the principal means through which incomes are redistributed to meet a range of circumstances and contingencies including retirement, widowhood, invalidity, sickness, unemployment, lone parenthood and costs of children.

The first question considered was who was receiving social security benefits of one kind or another. Over half of all families were normally receiving social security of one kind or another, as shown in Table 4.1. Only among the childless, non-elderly did a minority receive social security; even in the highest income levels 30 per cent received some form of benefit.

The average amounts received varied greatly by type of family, as shown in Table 4.2, but the overall gains to the worst off families were much greater than to the better off families. Supplementary Benefit was, not surprisingly, most selective but even Child Benefit gave more benefit to most low income groups than to the better off groups (as well, of course, as giving most benefit to larger families).

The distribution of benefits by type of family and income level is shown in Table 4.3. Half of all social security goes to the three lowest income groups (under 120 per cent of SB) which comprise one quarter of all families. Supplementary Benefit is most selective and Sickness and Industrial Injury Benefits least selective.

The ratio of gross social security to total net incomes is shown in Table 4.4. For the elderly only those above twice SB level received on average less than half their net income from social security; overall it provided about three-quarters of their income. For most other types of family at the lowest income levels social security amounted to more than half of net income. Only for non-elderly couples with less than four children did social security on average amount to less than one-tenth of net income.

Studies of income distribution tend for simplicity to concentrate on numbers or proportions falling below certain income levels. Beckerman stressed the importance of considering how far people fall below the specified level (Beckerman, 1979). He did this by calculating 'poverty gaps' - the average amount by which those below a specified poverty level fall below the level. This work has been replicated with the results shown in Table 4.5. Poverty gaps have been estimated both including and excluding social security income.

Average poverty gaps which under existing policies are greatest for large and one-parent families would, in the absence of social security, be enormously increased. Without social security one-quarter of all families would fall below 50 per cent of SB level. Social security is not, therefore, wholly effective in preventing poverty but it is highly effective in reducing it.

TABLE 4.1

Proportion of familes receiving social security benefits

Percentages

Type of family	All social security benefits	Supplementary benefit	Retirement benefit (a)	Widow's pension	Invalid pension	Sickness & ind.inj. benefits (b)	Unempl. benefit (b)	Child benefit (c)	Family income supplement (c)
Elderly couple	98.8	14.7	98.1	-	-	-	-	-	-
Elderly man	97.4	27.4	96.3	-	-	-	-	-	-
Elderly woman	98.9	38.2	92.0	5.1	-	-	-	-	-
Couple, no children	20.2	2.4	-	-	0.7	3.3	2.4	-	0.3
Couple, 1 child	73.5	1.1	-	-	1.9	2.3	3.0	68.6	0.4
Couple, 2 children	97.1	2.1	-	-	0.3	1.7	2.6	96.6	0.3
Couple, 3 children	99.2	3.0	-	-	-	2.2	2.7	99.2	0.3
Couple, 4 children	99.3	9.0	-	-	-	4.5	5.2	99.3	2.2
Couple, 5+ children	100.0	12.8	-	-	-	2.1	6.4	100.0	6.4
Lone parent, 1+ child	93.6	41.7	-	15.9	-	0.3	2.0	85.4	1.4
Single man	12.1	5.3	-	-	-	1.7	3.9	-	-
Single woman	23.0	7.0	-	12.0	0.1	0.7	3.1	-	-
Family normal income as % of SB level									
Under 90	76.2	36.9	90.8	2.9	0.2	1.2	13.0	81.8	0.7
90-	89.2	26.7	96.3	4.7	-	1.6	12.0	82.9	1.2
100-	88.0	42.5	96.5	3.2	0.1	1.7	4.9	89.7	4.1
120-	71.2	9.5	96.5	2.8	-	0.6	3.5	86.8	2.1
140-	58.5	2.0	93.1	2.3	0.2	1.1	1.9	89.6	0.3
200-	47.1	0.5	91.7	2.1	0.9	2.3	1.5	87.0	-
300-	30.5	0.6	85.7	2.0	0.3	4.1	1.7	84.0	-
500-	30.3	-	90.0	1.8	-	2.1	4.1	58.5	-
Total	58.5	10.6	94.7	2.5	0.4	2.0	3.0	87.0	0.6

(a) Families with elderly heads only
(b) Families with non-elderly heads only
(c) Families with children only

TABLE 4.2

Mean amounts of social security benefits received

£ per week

Type of family	All social security benefits	Supplementary benefit	Retirement benefit (a)	Widow's pension	Invalid pension	Sickness & ind.inj. benefits (b)	Unempl. benefit (b)	Child benefit (c)	Family income supplement (c)
Elderly couple	27.16	1.00	25.44	-	-	-	-	-	-
Elderly man	17.38	1.46	15.36	-	-	-	-	-	-
Elderly woman	18.10	2.56	14.31	.81	-	-	-	-	-
Couple, no children	4.31	.40	-	-	.12	.68	.50	-	-
Couple, 1 child	3.17	.29	-	-	.31	.60	.76	0.70	.02
Couple, 2 children	4.12	.57	-	-	.05	.45	.78	2.14	.02
Couple, 3 children	6.32	1.11	-	-	-	.61	.77	3.67	.01
Couple, 4 children	12.73	2.76	-	-	-	1.44	2.09	5.10	.09
Couple, 5+ children	21.70	5.60	-	-	-	.81	2.99	7.38	.61
Lone parent, 1+ child	17.26	9.94	-	4.28	-	.10	.40	2.04	.14
Single man	1.92	.61	-	-	-	.25	.64	-	-
Single woman	3.47	.72	-	1.76	.01	.08	.38	-	-
Family normal income as % of SB level									
Under 90	12.91	5.75	14.91	.42	.02	.17	2.06	2.07	.17
90-	18.21	3.83	16.78	.73	-	.29	3.43	2.70	.18
100-	18.35	3.60	18.11	.58	-	.38	1.22	2.57	.24
120-	12.09	1.04	20.04	.57	-	.10	.80	2.35	.14
140-	6.43	.28	19.79	.43	.03	.26	.45	2.28	.01
200-	4.01	.09	19.38	.35	.15	.55	.31	1.81	-
300-	3.11	.12	16.70	.34	.07	.84	.34	1.75	-
500-	4.07	-	18.85	.36	-	.46	1.00	1.33	-
Total	8.27	1.21	18.35	.44	.06	.45	.64	2.09	.05

(a), (b), (c): See Table 4.1

TABLE 4.3

Distribution of social security benefits

Percentages

Type of family	All social security benefits	Supplementary benefit	Retirement benefit	Widow's pension	Invalid pension	Sickness & ind.inj. benefits	Unempl. benefit	Child benefit	Family income supplement	All families
			(a)			(b)	(b)	(c)	(c)	
Elderly couple	26.2	6.6	48.6	–	–	–	–	–	–	8.0
Elderly man	6.2	3.6	10.9	–	–	–	–	–	–	3.0
Elderly woman	25.9	25.1	40.6	21.7	–	–	–	–	–	11.8
Couple, no children	10.3	6.5	–	–	39.5	38.8	19.8	–	–	19.7
Couple, 1 child	3.8	2.3	–	–	49.4	17.0	15.2	10.8	13.9	9.9
Couple, 2 children	5.8	5.5	–	–	8.7	15.3	18.5	38.8	18.4	11.7
Couple, 3 children	3.0	3.7	–	–	–	7.0	6.2	22.7	3.5	4.0
Couple, 4 children	2.3	3.3	–	–	–	6.1	6.2	11.6	9.8	1.5
Couple, 5+ children	1.3	2.4	–	–	–	1.2	3.1	5.9	22.3	.5
Lone parent, 1+ child	6.7	26.5	–	31.4	–	0.9	2.6	10.2	32.2	3.2
Single man	3.5	7.6	–	–	–	10.8	19.5	–	–	15.1
Single woman	4.9	6.9	–	46.8	2.3	2.8	9.0	–	–	11.7
Family normal income as % of SB level										
Under 90	10.0	30.4	6.0	6.0	2.3	2.4	19.5	4.8	17.7	6.4
90–	10.3	14.8	10.7	7.8	–	1.7	13.8	3.7	11.2	4.7
100–	28.6	38.3	36.6	16.9	1.2	4.8	10.9	8.5	36.5	12.9
120–	12.5	7.3	15.1	11.0	–	1.6	8.7	9.4	24.6	8.5
140–	19.7	5.9	19.6	24.6	14.1	15.8	19.4	37.0	10.0	25.3
200–	12.9	1.9	8.0	21.2	66.1	39.7	15.6	28.0	–	26.5
300–	5.2	1.4	3.1	10.8	16.3	32.0	8.9	7.8	–	13.9
500–	0.9	–	1.0	1.5	–	2.1	3.2	0.9	–	1.8
Total	100	100	100	100	100	100	100	100	100	100

(a), (b), (c): See Table 4.1

TABLE 4.4

Social security as proportion of total net income

Percentages

Type of family	Family normal income as % of SB level								All incomes
	Under 90	90-	100-	120-	140-	200-	300-	500+	
Elderly couple	88.8*	91.1	86.2	73.2	56.7	37.5	20.5	14.0*	67.4
Elderly man	93.8	87.4	89.0	74.0	54.4	29.5	25.6	10.2*	72.0
Elderly woman	89.8	89.6	89.3	70.6	54.5	37.2	24.6	12.2*	78.3
Couple, no children	44.3	82.9	57.0	29.9	11.2	4.6	2.2	0.3	9.2
Couple, 1 child	54.9	32.7*	26.1	3.3	3.1	3.1	2.3	2.1*	5.7
Couple, 2 children	50.4	59.0*	19.0	7.9	4.1	3.7	1.6	1.6*	6.8
Couple, 3 children	44.5	38.1*	24.9	8.7	7.1	4.5	3.6	1.3*	9.1
Couple, 4 children	51.3*	77.2*	38.5*	19.5*	7.7	10.8	2.5*	-	20.6
Couple, 5+ children	69.4*	80.3*	15.1*	44.9*	13.6*	4.6*	2.9*	-	30.6
Lone parent, 1+ child	77.3	81.1	75.5	49.9	20.1	13.4	8.9*	7.3*	49.4
Single man	59.8	47.4	24.8	16.7	3.4	1.3	1.0	0.0	10.0
Single woman	53.0	45.4	26.5	12.0	5.4	5.8	5.4	2.0*	15.6
Total	65.9	77.2	69.7	37.0	14.3	6.0	3.4	2.3	25.7

* Indicates base of less than 20.

TABLE 4.5

POVERTY GAPS

Type of family	Mean gap below SB level		Proportion below:					
			50% of SB level		SB level		140% of SB level	
	with soc.sec.	without soc.sec.	with soc.sec.	without soc.sec.	with soc.sec.	without soc.sec.	with soc.sec.	without soc.sec.
	£ p.w.	£ p.w.	%	%	%	%	%	%
Elderly couple	.17	16.97		67.3	8.2	84.1	56.8	88.9
Elderly man	.37	12.87		77.0	18.9	85.9	68.5	89.2
Elderly woman	.49	14.98		83.2	26.4	91.1	79.2	93.4
Couple, no children	.18	1.90		7.1	3.5	10.0	10.2	15.2
Couple, 1 child	.23	1.28		3.6	3.7	6.1	14.8	17.1
Couple, 2 children	.35	1.67		4.1	4.0	7.3	17.0	21.0
Couple, 3 children	.39	2.13		4.4	4.1	10.4	24.0	33.1
Couple, 4 children	1.17	8.08		15.6	14.2	27.5	38.0	43.9
Couple, 5+ children	1.59	16.60		23.4	23.4	38.3	44.6	55.3
Lone parent, 1+ child	1.48	14.40		49.1	32.9	61.0	58.3	72.2
Single man	.60	2.07		11.6	11.2	14.9	21.7	23.0
Single woman	.92	3.00		17.3	16.7	24.3	35.8	40.2
Total	.47	5.62	1.0	25.6	11.1	31.5	32.5	40.7

PART II - SIMULATION

Chapter 5

Minimum Wage

The relationship between the distribution of incomes and the labour market was considered in Chapter 3. There are many policies affecting the labour-market that would have major distributional effects. Most important, policies that affect the level of unemployment in turn affect incomes. There are, however, problems in simulating the effects of reducing - or increasing - the level of unemployment: data on past earnings becomes less reliable as duration of unemployment increases, particularly as a guide to future earnings, and the information collected in the Family Expenditure Survey is not adequate to make useful estimates of the effects on income distribution of changed levels of unemployment. Other labour market changes affecting older workers and married women are considered in the next two chapters.

In this chapter one policy - a minimum wage - will be considered in a variety of forms and on different assumptions. A legally enforced minimum wage has been widely proposed as a remedy for low pay and to reduce poverty. The purpose here is not to evaluate its likely effectiveness in reducing low pay nor to estimate labour supply responses. The purpose is to illustrate the effects of changed rates of pay on the overall distribution of incomes, assuming it has been enforced.

In Part A the minimum wage policies that have been considered are described. In Part B the results are presented assuming no labour demand effects. In Part C the effects with illustrative labour demand responses are described.

A. Minimum wage policies

Any feasible minimum wage policy would have to be based on hourly earnings. Here three variants of a minimum wage are considered:

a)   a minimum wage of 75 pence per hour such that all those with hourly earnings below 75 pence per hour increased their hourly earnings up to 75 pence.

b)   a minimum wage of 100 pence per hour such that all those with hourly earnings below 100 pence increased them to 100 pence.

c)   a minimum wage of 100 pence per hour which has repercussions affecting those with hourly earnings above 100 pence per hour.   The assumption has been made that those with hourly earnings under 75 pence increased them to 100 pence but those with hourly earnings between 75 pence and 125 pence are assumed to increase hourly earnings by half the difference between 125 pence and actual hourly earnings.   For example an individual on 85 pence per hour would, on this assumption, move up to 105 pence an hour; someone on 105 pence would move up to 115 pence.   This variant is therefore intended to illustrate the effects of the repercussions that might very well arise with the introduction of a minimum wage.

For comparison, in April 1977 the average hourly earnings of full-time adult manual workers was for men 156.5 pence and for women 111.2 pence; the proportions of these workers earning under 100 pence per hour were 3.2 per cent of men and 34.0 per cent of women (Department of Employment, 1977).

These three variants have been considered applying to:

i)   all workers

ii)   all workers aged 21 and over.

The effect of the minimum wage is calculated for each individual by multiplying the increase in hourly earnings, if any, by normal weekly hours.   Where there were no recorded hours or hourly earnings for an individual, the minimum wage was assumed to have no effect on that individual.   Effects were calculated separately for heads of families and for spouses and, to obtain the effect on family income, the gains, if any, were added.   In this way, the gross effect of the three variants on a minimum wage were estimated.

Having calculated the gross effect a series of adjustments were made.

First an adjustment was made for income tax and national insurance contributions. All workers were assumed to pay earnings-related national insurance contributions of 5.75 per cent on any gross gain.   Those, and only those, already paying income

tax in their family were assumed to pay tax on any gross gain from a minimum wage
at the standard rate then prevailing of 34 per cent.   These adjustments involve
simplifications which involve minor errors but these are unlikely to have any
material effect on the results: some married women would not be paying the full
national insurance contribution and where the woman had low gross earnings she
might not be paying income tax even though her husband was; some who were not
previously paying income tax would, with the gain from minimum wage, move into
income tax.   None of these discrepancies could, given the data, have been
rectified with complete accuracy and the complexity of making the attempt was not
considered justifiable.

The second major adjustment was to the price level.   Since a minimum wage
would increase the cost of labour it would almost inevitably result in higher
prices.   Some writers have suggested that a minimum wage would lead to productivity
increases sufficient to prevent prices rising but here it is assumed that the
minimum wage policy would be a zero sum game - gains to some would be precisely
offset by losses to others.   It has been calculated for each minimum wage
variant how much prices would have to rise so that the aggregate net effect was
zero.   (Price rises affect of course not merely the gains from a minimum wage
but also the real value of everyone's total income).

The price adjustments made with each variant of a minimum wage are shown in
Table 5.1 along with the aggregated gross cost and after tax cost of the minimum
wage for Great Britain in 1977.   This aggregation was based on the overall
sampling fraction achieved in the Family Expenditure Survey.

B.   Minimum wage effects (with no labour supply effect)

Overall 8 per cent of families would have one or more members directly
affected by a general minimum wage of 75 pence per hour, 21 per cent by a 100
pence minimum, and 37 per cent by a minimum of 100 pence with repercussions.

If the minimum wage were restricted to adults (those 21 or over) the proportions affected would be 4, 15 and 29 per cent respectively. The proportion of families directly affected are shown by income level in Table 5.2; they are lowest in the highest income level, as is to be expected, and also in the lowest income level.

The proportions affected and average effect are shown by type of family in Table 5.3 for a minimum of 100 pence for all and for adults (the two policies on which attention is particularly focussed). It is single people with and without children and spouses who are most affected, although if the minimum is restricted to adults the gains to single men and women are greatly reduced. The differential impact by age is shown in Table 5.4: the 100 pence minimum for all would on average produce a very large gain to families - mostly single people - where the head is aged under 21; all other age groups would on average lose. This age effect is transformed if the minimum wage is confined to adults.

In relation to family income level, the average losses are greatest at the highest income level, as shown in Table 5.5, but the average gains are not greatest in the lowest income level. This result is an amalgamation of the individual effects particularly on single people and spouses. These are set out for the general 100 pence minimum in Tables 5.6 and 5.7 and for 100 pence minimum for adults in Tables 5.9 and 5.10.

The use of the proportion affected and the mean gain as indicators of the distributional effect inevitably conceals the disparity of effects. Some may gain substantially from a minimum wage, others through the price effect may lose lesser amounts. In Tables 5.8 and 5.11 the distribution of incomes before and after each minimum is shown. Initially 11.1 per cent of families had a family income below SB level. With a minimum wage of 100 pence for all, that proportion rises to 11.7 per cent. Of those initially under SB level, some of course rise above SB level, indeed some above 200 per cent of SB level. Nevertheless the

simulated effect is of an overall increase in the number of families below SB
level.   On the other hand the proportion below 140 per cent of SB level falls
from 32.5 per cent to 29.9 per cent.   A similar, although less marked, effect
results from a 100 pence minimum for adults only.

The effects of all six minimum wage policies are summarised in Table 5.12.
Only the 75 pence minimum for all reduces the proportion below SB level; it
benefits those with the lowest hourly earnings and does not have a large price
effect.   All the other minimum wages simulated increase the proportion below
SB level, by one per cent in the case of a 100 pence minimum with repercussions.
By contrast, the proportion below 140 per cent of SB level is reduced by all the
policies.   All the policies reduce the Gini coefficient but the effects on the
Atkinson measure are variable: if alpha is -2.0, all the policies reduce equality;
if alpha is -1.0 or - 0.5, all three minimum wages for all increase equality but
the effect of the minimum wage for adults depends on the level of the minimum
wage.

C.   Effects with Labour Demand Response

A labour demand effect has been simulated for illustrative purposes.   It
has often been contended that a minimum wage would lead to unemployment amongst
those affected.   No attempt is made here to estimate the extent of any such
unemployment but the effects are simulated of 10 per cent and 20 per cent
unemployment amongst those directly affected by the minimum wage.   Unemployment
is randomly assigned to one in ten or one in five of those affected by the
minimum wage; those "becoming" unemployed are assumed to lose their normal take
home pay but, if they are head of family, they instead receive the appropriate
short-term Supplementary Benefit level for their family. No allowance has been
made for the cost of financing the increased social security benefits.   No
different price assumption has been estimated so that with the resulting losses of
income there is an overall mean loss of 34 pence per week with 10 per cent unemployment
with a 100 pence minimum for all. The distribution of the effects by income level

of allowing for unemployment are shown in Table 5.13.   In the lowest income
levels the effect of the assumed unemployment is relatively slight: this is
because the supplementary benefit which is assigned to the families replaces
most of the lost earnings and sometimes even exceeds those earnings.   The
biggest effect of the unemployment is seen in the middle income levels;
unemployment resulting from the minimum wage is most prevalent amongst spouses
who are assumed to lose their earnings with no social security replacement.

Allowing for 10 per cent unemployment increases the proportion below SB
level after a 100 pence minimum for all to 12.4 per cent but there is still a
reduction in the proportion below 140 per cent of SB level, as shown in Table
5.14.   The effects of different unemployment assumptions are summarised in
Table 5.15.   With 10 per cent unemployment, only with a 100 pence minimum for
all and if alpha is -0.5 is the Atkinson equality measure increased; in all
other cases equality is reduced.   With 20 per cent unemployment, equality is
in all cases reduced.

The distributional effects of a minimum wage would of course be altered if
the assumed price effect were off-set for certain groups, for example through
the indexation of social security benefits.   Such a combination of policy changes
is considered in Chapter 9.

TABLE 5.1

Costs and price adjustment of minimum wage

Minimum wage	Gross £m. p.a.	After tax £m. p.a.	Net of tax and price adjustment	Price adjustment %
For all				
75p	623	455	0	0.48
100p	2283	1579	0	1.66
100p+ repercussions	3380	2273	0	2.37
For adults				
75p	295	203	0	0.22
100p	1253	833	0	0.88
100p+ repercussions	2160	1408	0	1.48

TABLE 5.2

Proportion of families directly affected by minimum wage

Percentages

Income as percentage of SB level	For all			For adults		
	75p	100p	100p + REP	75p	100p	100p + REP
Under 100	7.1	9.7	11.0	2.1	4.2	5.4
100-	12.5	19.6	26.4	4.2	9.2	15.7
140-	8.9	30.8	51.9	6.5	21.2	37.0
200-	5.6	23.5	47.0	5.1	21.7	43.6
300+	2.1	10.3	26.1	2.0	9.9	25.1
All	7.5	20.9	36.6	4.4	15.1	28.8

TABLE 5.3

Effects of minimum wage by type of family

	100p MW for all		100p MW for adults	
	Proportion directly affected	Mean change	Proportion directly affected	Mean change
	%	pence p.w.	%	pence p.w.
Single man	24.0	+104	5.7	- 6
woman	36.4	+187	12.8	+14
Couple no children				
Husband	3.1	-122	3.1	-60
Wife	21.3	+ 64	20.3	+59
Total	23.3	- 58	22.2	- 1
Couple with children				
Husband	2.9	-125	2.9	-58
Wife	21.8	+ 60	21.6	+60
Total	23.9	- 65	23.7	+ 2
Lone parent				
with children	18.3	+ 2	16.9	+27
Elderly	5.7	- 35	5.7	- 9
All	20.9	-	15.1	-

TABLE 5.4

Effects of minimum wage by age

Mean gain or loss in pence per week

	100p MW for all	100p MW for adults
Age of family head		
Under 21	+404	-25
21-	- 7	+24
25-	- 58	+ 2
55-	- 35	+12
65 and over	- 38	-11
All ages	-	-

TABLE 5.5

Effects of 100p minimum wage for all and for adults by income level

Mean gain or loss in pence per week

	100p MW for all	100p MW for adults
Family normal income as percentage of SB level		
Under 100	+ 68	+ 5
100-	+ 91	+11
140-	+ 34	+29
200-	- 46	-
300+	-149	-65
All	-	-

TABLE 5.6

Proportion of families directly affected by 100 pence/hour minimum wage for all

Percentages

Family normal income as percentage of SB level	Single man	Single woman	Couple no children			Couple with children			Single parent with children	Elderly	All
			Husband	Spouse	Total	Husband	Spouse	Total			
Under 100	14.3	25.1	-	6.3	6.3	6.6	8.2	13.1	8.2	0.8	9.7
100-	65.3	71.1	5.0	10.8	15.0	8.2	13.8	20.0	30.7	3.0	19.6
140-	48.1	48.9	5.5	20.6	24.1	2.7	24.9	26.7	21.1	16.4	30.8
200-	9.8	12.9	4.0	32.1	34.1	1.3	27.4	28.2	20.0	11.5	23.5
300+	2.1	3.8	0.9	14.5	15.4	0.3	11.3	11.7	-	3.3	10.3
All	24.0	36.4	3.1	21.3	23.3	2.9	21.8	23.9	18.3	5.7	20.9

TABLE 5.7

Effects of 100 pence/hour minimum wage for all
Mean gain or loss in pence per week

Family normal income as percentage of SB level	Single man	Single woman	Couple no children			Couple with children			Single parent with children	Elderly	All
			Husband	Spouse	Total	Husband	Spouse	Total			
Under 100	+173	+315	- 44	+11	- 33	- 37	+16	- 21	+ 26	- 32	+ 68
100-	+663	+569	- 47	+26	- 21	- 37	+36	- 1	+ 66	- 34	+ 91
140-	+176	+124	- 61	+72	+ 11	-101	+75	- 26	- 24	- 6	+ 34
200-	- 20	- 13	-109	+99	- 10	-152	+61	- 91	- 78	- 54	- 46
300+	-104	-107	-185	+37	-148	-259	+58	-201	-195	-165	-149
All	+104	+187	-122	+64	- 58	-125	+60	- 65	+ 2	- 35	0

TABLE 5.8

Effect of 100 pence minimum wage for all on income distribution

Percentages

	Initial Distribution*					
	Under 100	100-	140-	200-	300-	All
Distribution* adjusted for net effect of minimum wage						
Under 100	10.3	1.4	-	-	-	11.7
100-	0.2	17.2	0.8	-	-	18.2
140-	0.4	2.3	23.1	0.9	-	26.7
200-	0.2	0.5	1.4	25.3	1.0	28.5
300+	-	-	-	0.3	14.7	15.0
All	11.1	21.4	25.3	26.5	15.7	100

* Distribution of Family Normal Income as percentage of SB level.

TABLE 5.9

Proportion of families directly affected by 100 pence/hour minimum wage for adults

Percentages

Family normal income as percentage of SB level	Single man	Single woman	Couple no children			Couple with children			Single parent with children	Elderly	All
			Husband	Spouse	Total	Husband	Spouse	Total			
Under 100	2.6	5.0	-	6.3	6.3	6.6	8.2	13.1	7.2	0.8	4.2
100-	4.9	16.2	5.0	10.0	14.2	8.2	13.5	19.7	28.0	3.0	9.2
140-	12.0	20.7	5.5	19.6	23.2	2.7	24.6	26.4	19.7	16.4	21.2
200-	5.2	8.9	4.0	30.2	32.3	1.3	27.2	28.1	20.0	11.5	21.7
300+	1.1	3.8	0.9	14.0	14.9	0.3	11.3	11.7	-	3.3	9.9
All	5.7	12.8	3.1	20.3	22.2	2.9	21.6	23.7	16.9	5.7	15.1

TABLE 5.10

Effects of 100 pence/hour minimum wage for adults

Mean gain or loss in pence per week

Family normal income as percentage of SB level	Single man	Single women	Couple no children			Couple with children			Single parent with children	Elderly	All
			Husband	Spouse	Total	Husband	Spouse	Total			
Under 100	+15	+29	-24	+12	-12	- 6	+16	+11	+ 34	-16	+ 5
100-	+34	+51	-18	+15	- 3	+ 5	+36	+41	+ 81	-13	+11
140-	+22	+22	-21	+66	+46	- 44	+75	+30	+ 9	+27	+29
200-	-15	-10	-52	+92	+40	- 77	+61	-16	- 26	- 7	-
300+	-59	-50	-97	+35	-62	-137	+58	-79	-104	-82	-65
All	- 6	+14	-60	+59	- 1	- 58	+60	+ 2	+ 27	- 9	-

TABLE 5.11

Effect of 100 pence minimum wage for adults on income distribution

Percentages

	Initial distribution*					
	Under 100	100-	140-	200-	300-	All
Distribution* adjusted for net effect of minimum wage						
Under 100	10.8	0.7	-	-	-	11.4
100-	0.1	20.0	0.5	-	-	20.6
140-	0.1	0.7	23.9	0.5	-	25.2
200-	-	-	0.9	25.7	0.7	27.4
300+	-	-	-	0.3	14.9	15.2
All	11.1	21.4	25.3	26.5	15.7	100

* Distribution of family normal income as percentage of SB level.

TABLE 5.12

Summary of effects of minimum wages

	Initial distribution	For all			For adults		
		75p	100p	100p + REP	75p	100p	100p + REP
Proportion below:							
SB level	11.1%	10.9%	11.7%	12.1%	11.2%	11.4%	12.0%
140% of SB level	32.5%	31.2%	29.9%	29.7%	32.2%	32.0%	32.1%
5th percentile	0.86	0.86	0.85	0.84	0.86	0.85	0.85
Lowest decile	0.98	0.98	0.97	0.96	0.98	0.97	0.97
Lower quantile	1.22	1.25	1.25	1.25	1.22	1.22	1.22
Median	1.81	1.82	1.85	1.87	1.82	1.83	1.84
Upper quantile	2.57	2.56	2.56	2.57	2.56	2.57	2.58
Highest decile	3.36	3.35	3.32	3.31	3.35	3.35	3.34
95th percentile	3.93	3.91	3.88	3.85	3.92	3.90	3.89
Gini coefficient	.280	.277	.273	.272	.279	.279	.279
Atkinson measure							
$\alpha = -0.5$	.8272	.8308	.8319	.8314	.8278	.8276	.8269
$\alpha = -1.0$	.7453	.7492	.7488	.7472	.7460	.7451	.7436
$\alpha = -2.0$	.3539	.3530	.3479	.3447	.3535	.3510	.3485

TABLE 5.13

Effect of minimum wages allowing for unemployment

Mean gain or loss in pence per week

Family normal income as % of SB level	100p MW for all net effect unemployment			100p MW for adults net effect unemployment		
	Nil	10%	20%	Nil	10%	20%
Under 100	+ 68	+ 58	+ 43	+ 5	-	-
100-	+ 91	+ 70	+ 37	+11	+ 7	- 3
140-	+ 34	- 22	- 54	+29	- 7	- 29
200-	- 46	- 82	-134	-	-35	- 79
300 and over	-149	-179	-200	-65	-94	-113
Total	-	- 34	-68	-	-24	- 47

TABLE 5.14

Effect of 100 pence minimum wage for all on income distribution
Allowing for 10% unemployment

Initial distribution

Percentages

	Under 100	100-	140-	200-	300 and over	All
Distribution adjusted for net effect of minimum wage allowing for 10% unemployment						
Under 100	10.4	1.7	0.4	-	-	12.4
100-	0.1	17.2	1.0	-	-	18.4
140-	0.3	2.1	22.6	1.2	-	26.2
200-	0.2	0.4	1.3	25.0	1.2	28.1
300 and over	-	-	-	0.3	14.4	14.8
All	11.1	21.4	25.3	26.5	15.7	100

TABLE 5.15

Effects of minimum wages allowing for unemployment

	Initial distribution	100p for all unemployment			100p for adults unemployment		
		Nil	10%	20%	Nil	10%	20%
Proportion below:							
SB level	11.1%	11.7%	12.4%	13.1%	11.4%	11.7%	11.9%
140% of SB level	32.5%	29.9%	30.8%	31.7%	32.0%	32.5%	32.9%
5th percentile	0.86	0.85	0.82	0.80	0.85	0.84	0.83
Lowest decile	0.98	0.97	0.96	0.95	0.97	0.97	0.96
Lower quantile	1.22	1.25	1.23	1.20	1.22	1.21	1.21
Median	1.81	1.85	1.83	1.82	1.83	1.81	1.80
Upper quantile	2.57	2.56	2.55	2.54	2.57	2.56	2.55
Highest decile	3.36	3.32	3.32	3.31	3.35	3.34	3.34
95th percentile	3.93	3.88	3.87	3.86	3.90	3.90	3.90
Gini coefficient	.280	.273	.277	.280	.279	.280	.281
Atkinson measure							
$\alpha = -0.5$	.8272	.8319	.8277	.8230	.8276	.8258	.8237
$\alpha = -1.0$	.7453	.7488	.7432	.7303	.7451	.7419	.7328
$\alpha = -2.0$	.3539	.3479	.3462	.2929	.3510	.3482	.3017

Chapter 6

Support for Children

The incidence of poverty increases with the number of children, as was seen in Chapter 2. This is not surprising since, even if incomes were similar for all families, those with more children have greater needs and are therefore likely to have lower income levels. Incomes are not, however, similar since the proportion of heads and spouses in paid work is related to number of children (Tables 3.1 and 3.2). While the analysis in Part I was mainly related to number of children, a factor of importance was the ages of the children. Most clearly, the presence of a very young child may affect the economic activity of one or both parents (see Table 3.3). The proportion of families at low income levels is shown in Table 6.1. While "needs", as defined by SB scale rates, increase with the age of the child, it is clear that low income levels are more common in families with one or more very young children.

Thus, in deciding which alternative child support policies to simulate, it was considered important to include a range of policies related to the age of children, to the size of family and to the presence of very young children. These policies are considered in Section A of this chapter. Given the known importance in two-parent families of the mother's earnings in maintaining the family income level, the effect of reducing or increasing the mother's earnings are considered in Section B. One purpose of these two sections is to allow a comparison to be made between the distributional effects of, on the one hand, cash benefits of various types and, on the other hand, policies for day care and nursery provision that may hinder or help mothers to work.

A. Cash benefits for families with children

Many proposals have been made for extending or modifying cash benefits for children. A selection from such proposals was made, as shown in Table 6.2. The first step was to simulate on the FES sample what each of these changes would cost. The second step was to adjust each change so that each of the five forms of change would have the same cost - £1,000 million per annum in 1977. The redistributional effects of these standardised increases, set out in Table 6.2, were then analyzed.

In this simulation no labour supply responses are allowed for. While there are studies which have assessed married women's labour supply responses (e.g. Greenhalgh, 1980, and Layard, Barton and Zabalza, 1980) these are not yet sufficiently sophisticated to identify responses to different forms of child support. No allowance for labour supply response has therefore been made. This assumption is probably not too misleading since the increases in child support considered would only represent a small proportion of a family's net income - although this is not to suggest labour supply responses may not be important and affect the distributional impact of any change. (Certain policy proposals, such as for a child care allowance conditional on a mother staying at home, would be likely to have much greater labour supply effects and for this reason, among others, they have not been considered.)

The average gains and losses for each of the standardised changes for each type of family and at each income level are shown in Table 6.3 and the effects are summarised in Table 6.4. The three types of Child Benefit increase described in Table 6.2 inevitably give more benefit to larger families than do the child care allowances. But the child care allowances add slightly more to those at low income levels and make the largest reductions in the proportion below 140 per cent of SB level. The size-related child benefit achieves the greatest reduction in Gini coefficient but the effects on the Atkinson measure vary with the value of alpha selected. Overall it appears that an age-related child benefit is somewhat less redistributive on all measures than the other changes. Apart from this no clear pattern emerges.

To compare the five child support measures in more detail, the analysis was restricted to families with children and then weighted by number of children, as shown in Table 6.5. Child care allowances prove to be more effective in reducing the proportion of families with children which are at low income levels

but less effective than child benefit changes in reducing the proportion of
children who are in families at very low income levels.   There is not,
however, a great deal of difference in effectiveness between any of the policies;
all would have a sizeable impact on the extent to which children live at low
income levels.

B.   Changes in mothers' earnings

Simulating the effect of an increase in child benefit is, in principle at
least, quite straightforward; the policy change directly indicates the gain to
any particular family. With policies that affect the earnings of mothers two
problems arise. First, many mothers choose not to take paid employment and
therefore to simulate what would happen if they did earn would be to simulate
a situation which would not result from any conceivable policy change.   Second,
there is a problem in knowing how much earnings those who might choose to earn
would receive.

There are no perfect solutions to these problems and arbitrary assumptions
have had to be made.   First, it is assumed that changes in paid work only occur
for mothers where the youngest child is aged 2-4 years; it is these mothers
who are most likely to be influenced by changes in child care and nursery
provision.   Those with children under 2 are likely to remain severely restricted
in their ability to go out to work whereas those with older children may now
have the choice of taking paid employment.   Second, two effects on paid work
are considered.   Since it is known what mothers with a child aged 2-4 who were
doing paid work were earning, it is possible to simulate the result if all of
them had, through loss of child care facilities and other changes, to stop
earning.   The results of more women working cannot be simulated with similar
accuracy; the arbitrary change has been simulated of all these mothers earning
at least average hourly earnings for 20 hours per week, that is earning at
least £20 per week.

The results of these two simulations are shown in Tables 6.6 and 6.7.   If
the mothers with youngest child aged 2-4 stopped paid work the losses would

average (over all families with children) around £1 per week and would have a greater effect at higher income levels - in part because the inclusion of the mother's earnings raised the income level of the family.   The effect of all these mothers earning at least £20 would produce gains averaging around £3 for families with children.   Mothers stopping work would, predictably, increase the proportion below 140 per cent of SB level and would, less predictably, increase the inequality of income levels.   The extension of these mothers' earning would however do less to reduce the proportion at low income levels than the changes in child support simulated in Part A, which cost £1,000 million.

TABLE 6.1

Proportion of families below 140% of SB level by age of youngest child

Percentages

	Age of youngest child			
	Under 2	2-4	5-10	11 or over
Type of family				
Couple, 1 child	18.6	19.4	13.9	11.5
Couple, 2 children	26.8	18.4	13.3	13.2
Couple, 3+ children	32.6	40.3	23.7	19.2
Lone parent, 1+ children	89.5	82.4	47.3	46.0

TABLE 6.2

Changes in child support

	Initial assumption	Initial cost £m p.a.	Standardised increase (rounded)	Standardised cost £m p.a.
Flat-rate child benefit	£1 per child	955	£1.05 per child	1000
Age-related child benefit	£0.50 per child under 5 £1.00 " " 5-10 £1.50 " " 11 or over	1006	£0.50 per child under 5 £1.00 " " 5-10 £1.50 " " 11 or over	1000
Size-related child benefit	£2 per child excluding the first child	923	£2.20 per child excluding the first child	1000
Child care allowance A	£10 if youngest child under 5 £5 " " " 5-10	2768	£3.60 if youngest child under 5 £1.80 if youngest child 5-10	1000
Child care allowance B	£10 if youngest child under 2 £5 " " " 2-4	1419	£7 if youngest child under 2 £3.50 if youngest child 2-4	1000

TABLE 6.3

Effects of changes in child support

Mean gain in pence per week

	Child benefit	Age-related child benefit	Size-related child benefit	Child care allowance A	Child care allowance B
Type of family					
Couple, 1 child	105	100	-	177	208
Couple, 2 children	209	200	217	217	211
Couple, 3 children	314	324	433	234	204
Couple, 4 children	419	441	650	256	218
Couple, 5+ children	584	660	991	261	240
Lone parent, 1+ child	187	200	170	166	152
Family normal income as % of SB level					
Under 100	49	46	53	53	59
100-	51	49	57	51	56
140-	89	87	94	91	95
200-	68	71	60	67	60
300 and over	38	40	33	35	28

TABLE 6.4

Summary of effects of changes in child support

Proportion of families below:	Initial distribution	Child benefit			Child care allowance	
		Flat rate	Age-related	Size-related	A	B
S.B. level	11.1%	10.4%	10.4%	10.4%	10.4%	10.3%
140% of S.B. level	32.5%	31.6%	31.7%	31.6%	31.4%	31.2%
5th percentile	0.86	0.87	0.87	0.89	0.87	0.87
Lowest decile	0.98	0.99	0.99	1.06	1.99	0.99
Lower quartile	1.22	1.24	1.23	1.29	1.24	1.24
Median	1.81	1.84	1.84	1.83	1.84	1.84
Upper quartile	2.57	2.59	2.59	2.57	2.59	2.58
Highest decile	3.36	3.38	3.38	3.37	3.38	3.37
95th percentile	3.93	3.94	3.94	3.94	3.94	3.94
Gini coefficient	.280	.278	.278	.270	.277	.277
Atkinson measure						
$\alpha = -0.5$	.8272	.8284	.8277	.8385	.8306	.8306
$\alpha = -1.0$	.7453	.7455	.7432	.7576	.7511	.7503
$\alpha = -2.0$	.3539	.3469	.3390	.3517	.3573	.3549

TABLE 6.5

Effects of changes in child support

Percentages

	Initial distribution	Child benefit			Child care allowance	
		Flat rate	Age-related	Size-related	A	B
Proportion of all families below:						
SB level	11.1	10.4	10.4	10.4	10.4	10.3
140% of SB level	32.5	31.7	31.7	31.6	31.4	31.2
200% of SB level	57.8	56.9	56.9	56.9	56.7	56.5
Proportion of families with children below:						
SB level	7.8	5.9	5.8	5.9	5.8	5.6
140% of SB level	23.0	20.5	20.7	20.2	19.9	19.4
200% of SB level	56.9	54.0	53.9	54.0	53.5	53.2
Proportion of children in families below:						
SB level	8.5	5.7	5.7	5.0	6.6	6.4
140% of SB level	25.7	22.5	22.8	21.5	22.6	22.4
200% of SB level	61.5	58.0	57.9	57.5	58.3	58.3

TABLE 6.6

Effect of changes in paid work of married women
with youngest child aged 2-4

Type of family	All paid work stopped		All earn at least £20 per week	
	Proportion of Families Affected	Mean Effect	Proportion of Families Affected	Mean Effect
	%	pence p.w.	%	pence p.w.
Couple, 1 child	7.9	-101	14.2	+255
Couple, 2 children	11.1	-102	19.2	+330
Couple, 3 children	14.2	-166	21.3	+339
Couple, 4 children	13.4	-128	26.1	+434
Couple, 5+ children	10.6	- 94	23.4	+373
Family normal income as % of SB level				
Under 100	0.6	- 2	3.6	+ 73
100-	1.5	- 10	4.7	+ 85
140-	4.2	- 27	8.4	+141
200-	4.2	- 51	4.7	+ 75
300 and over	2.1	- 54	1.6	+ 29

TABLE 6.7

Effect of changes in paid work of married women
with youngest child aged 2-4

	Initial distribution	All paid work stopped	All earn at least £20 per week
Proportion below:			
S.B. level	11.1%	11.1%	10.6%
140% of SB level	32.5%	32.7%	31.2%
5th percentile	0.86	0.85	0.86
Lowest decile	0.98	0.98	0.99
Lower quantile	1.22	1.22	1.24
Median	1.81	1.80	1.86
Upper quantile	2.57	2.55	2.60
Highest decile	3.36	3.36	3.38
95th percentile	3.93	3.92	3.94
Gini coefficient	.280	.280	.278
Atkinson measure			
$\alpha = -0.5$	.8272	.8268	.8296
$\alpha = -1.0$	.7453	.7437	.7488
$\alpha = -2.0$	.3539	.3483	.3540

Chapter 7

Provision for the Elderly

The elderly have a high incidence of low income levels and constitute the largest group living at or close to SB levels. A very high proportion receive social security benefits and social security benefits amount to about three-quarters of their total net income; indeed well over half of all social security expenditure is on the elderly. The policy changes connected with the elderly that are simulated are, therefore, all connected with social security.

First, in Part A, increases in pension levels are simulated. Second, in Part B, another proposal that is frequently advocated is considered, namely the effect of lowering pensionable age for men to 60 years.

In these simulations the effects of allowing for predicted labour supply responses are taken into account. The predicted responses are taken from earlier work at the Centre for Labour Economics which investigated retirement behaviour (Zabalza and Piachaud, 1980).

A. Changes in pensions

Two variants of pension increases were considered. One involved raising the national insurance retirement pension that each person received and sub-jecting the increase to income tax. The limitation of this policy change is that those with little or no retirement pension who may receive supplementary benefit would appear to gain nothing. It is not possible to simulate the effect of raising supplementary benefit scale rates since the beneficiaries of such a change are not only those already receiving supplementary benefit (for whom the simulation presents no problem) but also those who become eligible for supplementary benefit; estimating who would be in the latter group presents severe problems. A simpler solution, which avoids these problems, is to assume flat-rate increases in net income for single and married elderly people; this is the second variant considered. The initial assumption and the standardised changes actually considered are shown in Table 7.1.

The predicted labour supply effect of pension increases of this magnitude is that two per cent of elderly workers would stop paid work (see Zabalza and Piachaud, 1980). (This effect is restricted in the simulation to men aged 65-74 and women aged 60-69.)

The results, with and without labour supply effects, of the two pension increases are shown in Tables 7.2 and 7.3. It is clear that there is little difference between the retirement pension increase and the across-the-board increase for all elderly families. Further, the predicted labour supply effect is so small as to make little difference. The gains are, of course, confined to elderly families and on average are of most benefit at low income levels.

The effect on the proportion below SB level is quite dramatic - a reduction from 11.1 per cent overall (including the non-elderly) to under 8 per cent. There is a less marked reduction in the proportion below 14.0 per cent of SB level. While Gini coefficients are in all cases reduced the effects on the Atkinson measures varies with the value of alpha; in all cases, however, the inclusion of labour supply effects reduces equality according to the Atkinson measure.

B.   Changes in pensionable age

Lowering the pensionable age for men to 60 years has frequently been advocated not only to provide longer retirement but also to equalise men's and women's pensionable ages and, more recently, to reduce unemployment. The simulation is restricted to lowering the pensionable age for men since this only involves men leaving paid work (raising the pensionable age involves assessing the effects of people entering paid work for whom there is the problem of estimating probable earnings). It has been assumed that men's pensions from age 60 would not be subject to any earnings rule.

Predicted labour supply effects would be very great: of men aged 60-64 it is predicted (Zabalza and Piachaud, 1980) that:

50 per cent would retire completely

20 per cent would move to part-time work (assumed to earn

one-third of previous earnings)

30 per cent would continue as before

These predicted economic states have been randomly assigned among men aged 60-64.

Since these labour supply effects are so large and, to a degree, uncertain, simulations have also been made assuming that there is no labour supply effect at all and assuming that all men over 60 stop all paid work. These two assumptions provide, in effect, the outer limits to what might result from lowering men's pensionable age.

The simulated effects are shown in Tables 7.4 and 7.5. The type of family most affected is the couple with no children; if all affected kept on earning there would be a substantial gain from receipt of pension but with the predicted labour supply response there would be, on average a loss. There is no clear pattern as to how these effects would be distributed between income levels. It is only with the summary measures (Table 7.5) that the effects become clearer. With the predicted labour supply response, incomes would fall and the proportion at low income levels would increase; with termination of labour supply this result would be more marked. If there were no labour supply effect, incomes, particularly of those in the upper quartile, would rise and equality in terms of the Atkinson measure would decline. With the predicted labour supply effect, the Atkinson measure would increase (i.e. more equality) with alpha at -0.5, reflecting a fall in high incomes, but with alpha at -1.0 or -2.0 it would fall due to the increase in low income families.

With existing levels of pension, a lowering of pensionable age for men to 60 would most probably mean a substantial fall in incomes for most men aged 60-64. However, while income may fall, it is important to remember that people who choose (and do not regret choosing) to stop working do not suffer a loss in their welfare.

TABLE 7.1

Changes in pensions

	Initial assumption	Initial cost	Standardised increase	Standardised cost
		£m. p.a.		£m. p.a.
Retirement pension	+10% - subject to tax	600	+16.7% - subject to tax	1000
Income of elderly	£1.00 single £1.60 couple	438	£2.30 single £3.65 couple	1000

TABLE 7.2

Effects of increases in pensions

Mean gain in pence per week

	No labour supply effect		With labour supply effect	
	Retirement pension	Income of elderly	Retirement pension	Income of elderly
Type of family				
Elderly couple	343	365	337	359
Elderly man	224	228	208	212
Elderly woman	212	228	212	228
All families	63	63	62	62
Family normal income as % of SB level				
Under 100	105	98	104	97
100-	157	148	157	148
140-	43	49	41	47
200-	17	19	15	18
300 and over	14	18	14	18

TABLE 7.3

Effects of increases in pensions

	Initial distribution	No labour supply effect		With labour supply effect	
		Retirement pension	Income of elderly	Retirement pension	Income of elderly
Proportion below:					
SB level	11.1%	7.7%	7.8%	7.7%	7.8%
140% of SB level	32.5%	30.4%	30.5%	30.5%	30.5%
5th percentile	0.86	0.89	0.89	0.89	0.89
Lowest decile	0.98	1.06	1.06	1.06	1.06
Lower quartile	1.22	1.30	1.29	1.30	1.29
Median	1.81	1.83	1.83	1.83	1.83
Upper quartile	2.57	2.57	2.57	2.57	2.57
Highest decile	3.36	3.37	3.37	3.37	3.37
95th percentile	3.93	3.94	3.94	3.94	3.94
Gini coefficient	.280	.269	.270	.269	.270
Atkinson measure					
$\alpha = -0.5$	.8272	.8397	.8385	.8382	.8378
$\alpha = -1.0$	.7453	.7590	.7576	.7547	.7564
$\alpha = -2.0$	.3539	.3522	.3517	.3454	.3511

TABLE 7.4

Effects of lowering pensionable age for men to 60

Mean gain or loss in pence per week

	No labour supply effect	Predicted labour supply effect	Termination of labour supply
Type of family			
Couple, no children	+334	-146	-380
All families	+ 81	- 33	- 87
Family normal income as % of SB level			
Under 100	+ 67	+ 52	+ 43
100-	+ 43	+ 18	+ 10
140-	+ 80	- 7	- 54
200-	+106	- 54	-135
300 and over	+104	-171	-283

TABLE 7.5

Effect of lowering pensionable age for men to 60

	Initial distribution	No labour supply effect	Predicted labour supply effect	Termination of labour supply
Proportion below:				
SB level	11.1%	10.2%	11.2%	11.7%
140% of SB level	32.5%	30.1%	32.7%	33.6%
5th percentile	0.86	0.86	0.84	0.83
Lowest decile	0.98	0.99	0.97	0.97
Lower quartile	1.22	1.23	1.21	1.20
Median	1.81	1.84	1.80	1.77
Upper quartile	2.57	2.62	2.56	2.53
Highest decile	3.36	3.41	3.35	3.32
95th percentile	3.93	4.01	3.92	3.89
Gini coefficient	.280	.281	.280	.281
Atkinson measure				
$\alpha = -0.5$	.8272	.8264	.8274	.8275
$\alpha = -1.0$	.7453	.7448	.7432	.7437
$\alpha = -2.0$	.3539	.3515	.3417	.3446

Chapter 8

Taxes - Positive and Negative

This chapter has two purposes. In preceding chapters increases in social security benefits have been considered: such changes have to be paid for with some form of additional revenue. The first purpose is, therefore, to consider the distribution of the burden of the most relevant taxes and the effect of changes in these taxes. The second purpose is to simulate the effects of various tax credit schemes and the consequences of a radical negative income tax.

A. Sources of revenue

The two forms of taxation that are considered here are national insurance contributions paid by employees and the self-employed (as opposed to employers' contributions) and personal income tax. These are of course many other forms of government taxation but their distributional impact is more complex than taxes on income. Even with these two forms of taxation of income there are problems in determining their incidence. Here it is only their immediate incidence that is analysed - how much each individual or family actually paid - and the questions of whether or to what extent wage rates are adjusted to take account of taxation are not considered.

The burden of N.I. contributions and income tax on different types of family and different income levels is shown in Table 8.1. Nearly three-quarters of families had one or more member paying income tax compared with 62 per cent paying NI contributions; the proportions paying each of these did not differ greatly for each type of family except for the elderly of whom only a small proportion paid NI contributions. In relation to income level, income tax bore much more heavily than NI contributions on the higher income levels but it also bore more heavily on the lowest income levels; this arises largely because of the concentration of the elderly in the lowest income levels.

Three methods of increasing revenue to finance benefit increases have been simulated. The first two are straightforward increases in the rates of NI contribution and of income tax, calculated so that the revenue would amount to £1,000 million per annum. The increase on NI contributions would have to be 25.0 per cent, equivalent to an increase from 5.75 per cent to 7.2 per cent on most earnings. On income tax the increase amounts to 5.5 per cent, equivalent to an extra 1.9 pence in the pound on standard rate and the same proportionally on higher rates of tax.

A possible source of extra revenue is lowering income tax allowances and thus the tax threshold; this has not been considered for two reasons. First, tax thresholds are already low and a deliberate reduction of the nominal allowances (as opposed to erosion of real allowances through inflation) is not a likely option. Second, there are technical difficulties in simulating the effects of lowering the tax threshold: no problem arises for those already paying income tax but estimating who would be brought into tax and how much they would pay requires detailed and accurate data on mortgage interest, pension contributions and other items allowable against tax; such data is not available therefore estimating the effect of a lower threshold would be subject to a wide margin of error.

The third source of revenue that has been simulated is the abolition of the married man's tax allowance; this would mean in effect lowering the married man's tax allowance to the level of a single person. Such a change has been increasingly advocated and would yield some £3 billion extra revenue (at 1977 prices). Estimating its effects is subject to the same problems as discussed in the last paragraph but since only married men are concerned this is less of a difficulty since the proportion of married men not already paying tax is lower than for other people.

The losses from each of the three sources of revenue are shown in Table 8.2 and the effects are summarised in Table 8.3. The incidence of higher NI contributions or income tax is, assuming no shifting, distributed in the same way as existing payments are now distributed. The income tax rate increase is the more progressive change in terms of the proportionate effect on the lowest and highest income levels. Increases in NI contributions and in the tax rate both increase equality in terms of the Gini coefficient and Atkinson measure; the abolition of the married man's allowance increases inequality on both measures.

Sources of revenue are not in isolation the principal focus of this study. Rather the concern is with revenue combined with changes in expenditure; such combinations are considered in Chapter 9.

B. Tax credits and negative income tax

The tax system has not solely been considered as a source of revenue. Countless schemes have been put forward to use the tax system as a redistributive mechanism - taking from those above certain income levels but also giving to those below these levels. The nearest any such scheme has come to implementation is Britain was the publication of a Green Paper on Tax Credits (HMSO, 1972); this proposal was for the replacement of personal tax allowances by tax credits which would, subject to certain conditions, have allowed some families on low incomes to receive net additions to their income throught the tax system. Although this proposal was not, for a variety of reasons, implemented, some form of tax credit is still canvassed as a possibility and it is of interest to simulate the redistributive effects.

The effect of the tax credit proposal is illustrated in Figure 8.1. In effect the tax credit extends the full value of the tax allowance (to the standard rate payer) to those below the tax threshold, thereby increasing their net income.

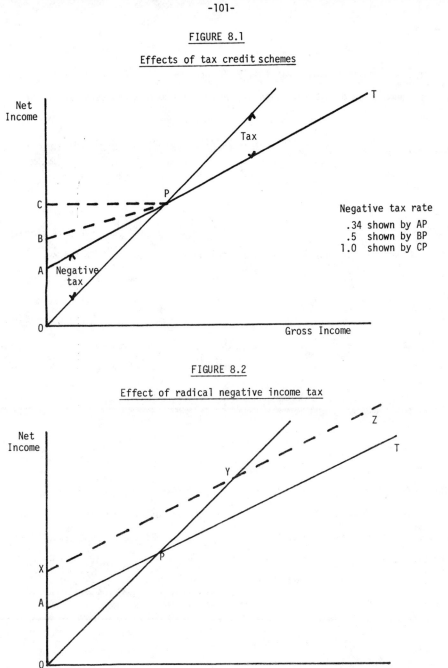

FIGURE 8.1

Effects of tax credit schemes

FIGURE 8.2

Effect of radical negative income tax

Thus the net income schedule, initially OPT becomes APT.   Other variants of such
a scheme have been put forward with higher negative tax rates, as shown in
Figure 8.1.   If the negative tax rate is 100 per cent (1.0) the net income
schedule is CPT; this means that any shortfall of income below the tax threshold
is fully made up; in effect the negative tax represents a floor or guaranteed
level of income.

The effects of three forms of negative tax or tax credit are shown in
Table 8.4 and 8.5.   The negative tax rate of 34 per cent (0.34) equal to standard
rate approximates as closely as possible to the 1973 proposal.   The higher rates
of 50 and 100 per cent represent more redistributive systems.   In simulating
these schemes the existing personal tax allowances (and age allowances) were
used.   It can be seen that the family types most affected were the elderly and
lone parents; in terms of income levels the effects were almost wholly concentrated
on those below 140 per cent of SB level and were highly selective.   The aggregate
cost of these schemes in 1977 would have been as follows:

Negative Tax Rate	Cost (£ million per annum)
.34	410
.5	605
1.0	1210

All three schemes would reduce the proportion of families below SB level
substantially; with the 100 per cent negative tax rate this proportion would be
halved.   However only with this 100 per cent rate would the proportion below 140
per cent of SB level fall substantially.   There are reductions in the Gini
coefficient and on the Atkinson measure equality is increased for all three
schemes for all values of alpha.   Thus these tax credit schemes are highly
selective and redistributive.

The tax credit or negative income tax schemes considered so far have been additions superimposed on the existing system of taxes and benefits. Some writers, notably Friedman (1962), have put forward a much more radical proposal - namely, that a negative income tax should replace the entire social security system and be the sole form of benefit. The arguments around this proposition have been set out elsewhere, for example in Sandford et. al. (1980). In this study a simulation has been carried out of the effects of implementing a radical negative income tax of the kind advocated by Friedman.

The policy of replacing all social security by a negative income tax has been simulated starting from the existing income distribution. In one way this is not a fair representation. Such a radical policy could scarcely, for reasons that will be seen, be introduced overnight; it is Friedman's argument that, in the absence of social security with, on his interpretation, its perverse effects, people could and would make satisfactory provision for themselves against the risks of inadequate income. But it is not known how people would respond to the total absence of social security. The purpose here of simulating a radical negative income tax is therefore to illustrate the direction of the effects, rather than to offer a realistic assessment of the effects of such a scheme introduced over a period of, perhaps, thirty or forty years.

It has been assumed, following Friedman, that the negative tax rate would not be set at a high rate since this would effect work inventives; the standard rate of 34 per cent is therefore used. The effects of this radical negative tax can be illustrated as shown in Figure 8.2. The effect can be divided into two components:

(1) that of introducing a tax credit, as shown by APT (corresponding to the same change in Table 8.1)

(2) that of abolishing social security and using the saving (net of the cost of (1)) to raise the tax threshold; this second component has the effect of

providing an equal gain to all families of a given size, irrespective of income, of an amount shown by AX.

The resulting net income schedule thus moves from the initial OPT to the final XYZ.   The levels of income guaranteed by the negative income tax, OX, on a zero net cost basis differ according to the tax threshold which varies with age and marital status, and are as follows:

	Elderly	Non-Elderly
Single Person	£ 8.17	£6.18
Married Couple	£12.91	£9.51

The effects of this radical negative income tax replacing social security are shown in Table 8.6 and 8.7.   On average the elderly and lone parents are losers and other family types gain.   Most strikingly, all the lowest income levels lose and the highest income levels gain.   The proportion under SB level would rise from 11 to 28 per cent and 20 per cent would be under 50 per cent of SB level.   Indeed most of those now under SB level would end up under half this level.   The summary of the effects in Table 8.7 shows that on all the measures inequality would be vastly increased.

The explanation for these effects is not hard to find.   The principal source of income at the lowest income levels - social security - is removed and replaced by a negative income tax worth far less.   In providing the negative income tax, tax thresholds are raised therefore benefiting better-off families.

Thus, as long as the elderly, lone parents and other groups now substantially dependent on social security have low original incomes (i.e. excluding state benefits), the replacement of social security by a comprehensive negative income tax system would have highly regressive effects.

There are of course variants of a radical negative income tax system with much higher rates of positive and negative tax.   These have not been simulated for two reasons.   First they do not conform with Friedman's proposals.   Second, a higher positive tax is what was simulated in Part A of this chapter; if the (positive) income tax rate were raised, the additional revenue could be used to finance any of the other benefit changes considered in preceding chapters.

In summary, while a tax credit scheme additional to the existing system of taxes and benefits would be highly selective and effective in reducing the number of families below SB level, the wholesale replacement of social security by a radical negative income tax would with the existing distribution of incomes, have highly regressive effects and greatly increase the numbers below, and far below, the SB level.

TABLE 8.1

Distribution of national insurance
contributions and income tax

	Proportion paying:		Mean amount		Proportion of total	
	NI contribution	Income tax	NI contribution	Income tax	NI contribution	Income tax
Type of family	%	%	£ p.w.	£ p.w.	%	%
Elderly couple	5.3	57.1	.10	5.02	0.3	3.5
Elderly man	2.2	38.1	.07	3.15	0.1	0.8
Elderly woman	1.1	33.0	.02	2.03	0.1	2.1
Couple, no children	84.5	90.9	4.11	18.87	32.1	32.3
Couple, 1 child	87.9	90.2	4.09	16.20	15.8	14.0
Couple, 2 children	85.4	90.1	4.04	17.03	18.8	17.3
Couple, 3 children	83.1	88.0	3.74	18.10	5.9	6.3
Couple, 4 children	73.9	76.9	3.39	12.63	2.0	1.6
Couple, 5+ children	70.2	66.0	3.32	12.40	0.7	0.6
Lone parent, 1+ child	38.6	39.3	.92	4.26	1.2	1.2
Single man	77.8	80.2	2.46	10.02	14.7	13.1
Single woman	72.1	77.3	1.77	7.13	8.2	7.3
Total	62.1	74.3	2.52	11.50	100	100
Family normal income as % of SB level						
Under 90	5.5	19.1	.09	.89	0.2	0.5
90-	9.8	18.7	.15	.61	0.3	0.2
100-	16.5	31.3	.37	1.06	1.9	1.2
120-	45.3	66.8	1.19	3.97	4.0	2.9
140-	74.6	87.5	2.51	8.89	25.2	19.6
200-	87.4	95.1	3.73	15.73	39.3	36.3
300-	87.1	96.6	4.79	25.81	26.4	31.2
500-	63.0	93.9	3.76	51.54	2.7	8.1
Total	62.1	74.3	2.52	11.50	100	100

TABLE 8.2

Effect of national insurance and income tax changes

Mean loss in pence per week

	Increase in NI contributions	Increase in tax rates	Abolition of married men's tax allowance
Type of family			
Elderly couple	- 3	- 27	-200
Elderly man	- 2	- 17	-
Elderly woman	- 1	- 11	-
Couple, no children	-103	-103	-377
Couple, 1 child	-100	- 89	-445
Couple, 2 children	-101	- 93	-444
Couple, 3 children	- 93	- 99	-481
Couple, 4 children	- 85	- 69	-545
Couple, 5+ children	- 83	- 68	-680
Lone parent, 1+ child	- 23	- 23	-
Single man	- 62	- 55	-
Single woman	- 44	- 39	-
Total	- 63	- 63	-217
Family normal income as % of SB level			
Under 100	- 3	- 4	- 76
100-	- 17	- 12	-126
140-	- 63	- 49	-239
200-	- 93	- 86	-272
300-	-117	-157	-314
Total	- 63	- 63	-217

TABLE 8.3

Effect of national insurance and income tax changes

	Initial distribution	Increase in NI contributions	Increase in Income tax rate	Abolition of married men's tax allowance
Proportion below:				
SB level	11.1%	11.2%	11.1%	12.9%
140% of SB level	32.5%	32.9%	32.8%	35.5%
5th percentile	0.86	0.85	0.85	0.81
Lowest decile	0.98	0.98	0.98	0.95
Lower quartile	1.22	1.21	1.21	1.17
Median	1.81	1.78	1.79	1.73
Upper quartile	2.57	2.53	2.53	2.47
Highest decile	3.36	3.31	3.30	3.26
95th percentile	3.93	3.88	3.88	3.84
Gini coefficient	.280	.279	.278	.283
Atkinson measure				
$\alpha = -0.5$	.8272	.8292	.8298	.8230
$\alpha = -1.0$	.7453	.7483	.7482	.7362
$\alpha = -2.0$	.3539	.3577	.3556	.3379

TABLE 8.4

Effects of tax credit schemes

	Proportion affected	Mean gain negative tax rate		
		.34	.5	1.0
Type of family	%	£ p.w.	£ p.w.	£ p.w.
Elderly couple	32.3	.72	1.06	2.12
Elderly man	44.1	.72	1.05	2.11
Elderly woman	50.5	.78	1.15	2.30
Couple, no children	1.6	.02	.03	.06
Couple, 1 child	0.8	.01	.02	.04
Couple, 2 children	0.5	.01	.02	.03
Couple, 3 children	0.3	.01	.02	.03
Couple, 4 children	0.7	.04	.05	.10
Couple, 5+ children	-	-	-	-
Lone parent, 1+ child	21.7	.52	.77	1.53
Single man	8.5	.18	.26	.52
Single woman	12.0	.29	.43	.86
Total	13.7	.26	.38	.76
Family normal income as % of SB level				
Under 90	65.8	1.70	2.50	4.99
90-	60.0	1.19	1.74	3.49
100-	44.8	.66	.97	1.94
120-	10.0	.09	.13	.27
140-	0.3	-	-	-
200-	-	-	-	-
300-	-	-	-	-
500-	-	-	-	-
Total	13.7	.26	.38	.76

TABLE 8.5

Effects of tax credit schemes

	Initial distribution	Negative tax rate		
		.34	.5	1.0
Proportion below:				
SB level	11.1%	8.2%	7.6%	5.5%
140% of SB level	32.5%	32.4%	32.4%	28.8%
5th percentile	0.86	0.89	0.91	0.98
Lowest decile	0.98	1.03	1.05	1.09
Lower quartile	1.22	1.24	1.26	1.34
Median	1.81	1.81	1.81	1.81
Upper quartile	2.57	2.57	2.57	2.57
Highest decile	3.36	3.36	3.36	3.36
95th percentile	3.93	3.93	3.93	3.93
Gini coefficient	.280	.273	.269	.260
Atkinson measure				
$\alpha = -0.5$	.8272	.8303	.8369	.8493
$\alpha = -1.0$	.7453	.7710	.7810	.7973
$\alpha = -2.0$	.3539	.5098	.5179	.5251

TABLE 8.6

Effect of replacing all social security with negative income tax

Type of family	Tax Gain	Loss of Soc.Sec.	Net Effect	Initial distribution proportion under SB level	Distribution with NIT replacing social security proportion under 50% of SB	SB level
	£ p.w.	£ p.w.	£ p.w.	%	%	%
Elderly couple	8.22	-27.16	-18.94	8.2	44.2	75.3
Elderly man	4.45	-17.38	-12.93	18.9	58.9	82.6
Elderly woman	4.52	-18.11	-13.59	26.4	73.6	88.4
Couple, no children	7.47	- 4.32	3.15	3.5	5.4	8.1
Couple, 1 child	11.18	- 3.17	8.01	3.7	3.0	4.2
Couple, 2 children	14.90	- 4.12	10.78	4.0.	3.3	4.5
Couple, 3 children	18.63	- 6.32	12.31	4.1	3.0	4.4
Couple, 4 children	22.37	-12.73	9.64	14.2	10.4	15.6
Couple, 5+ children	28.20	-21.70	6.50	23.4	19.1	23.4
Lone parent, 1+ child	10.88	-17.26	- 6.38	32.9	34.9	50.8
Single man	3.90	- 1.92	1.98	11.2	9.7	12.5
Single woman	4.02	- 3.47	.55	16.7	13.2	19.5
Total	8.27	- 8.27	-	11.1	20.2	27.7
Family normal income as % of SB level						
Under 90	8.03	-12.91	- 4.88	100	67.7	88.4
90-	7.59	-18.21	-10.62	100	80.6	85.3
100-	7.12	-18.34	-11.22	-	72.4	78.1
120-	8.17	-12.10	- 3.93	-	21.8	47.6
140-	9.10	- 6.44	2.66	-	3.3	14.9
200-	8.62	- 4.01	4.61	-	0.4	0.9
300-	7.61	- 3.11	4.50	-	0.1	0.1
500-	7.81	- 4.08	3.73	-	-	-
Total	8.27	- 8.27	-	11.1	20.2	27.7

TABLE 8.7

Effect of replacing all social security
by negative income tax

	Initial distribution	Social security replaced by N.I.T.
Proportion below:		
SB level	11.1%	27.7%
140% of SB level	32.5%	33.1%
5th percentile	0.86	0.09
Lowest decile	0.98	0.26
Lower quartile	1.22	0.74
Median	1.81	2.00
Upper quartile	2.57	2.76
Highest decile	3.36	3.58
95th percentile	3.93	4.16
Gini coefficients	.280	.384
Atkinson measure		
$\alpha = -0.5$	.8272	.5757
$\alpha = -1.0$	.7453	.2360
$\alpha = -2.0$	.3539	.0112

Chapter 9

Combined Policy Changes and Conclusions

In chapters 5-8 a variety of policy changes have been considered one at a time and compared with each other. This approach has the merit of clarifying the redistributive effects of each policy. But it is unrealistic in that it is impossible or unlikely for one policy change to be made in isolation. Most obviously this is true in the case of the changes in social security benefits which were standardised at a cost of £1000 million but compared without accounting for the source of this sum. Of course, almost any policy can be made to appear attractive and effective if it is assumed that the resources appear out of thin air. It is particularly important in assessing redistributional policies which are designed to combat poverty and reduce inequality that account be taken not just of who benefits but also of who pays. In this chapter some of the policy changes considered are summarised and then various combinations of policy changes are considered.

Most of the combined policies considered and compared in this chapter consist of combinations of the benefits for children and the elderly discussed in chapters 6 and 7 and methods of finance discussed in part A of chapter 8. Since there are literally dozens of such combinations - and an infinite number if the standardised £1000 million change is varied - a selection of the principal changes has been made all involving £1000 million extra expenditure and revenue.

First, however, in Table 9.1 the effects of different policies are summarised. Since for small changes the effects of each policy are approximately proportional to the size of the policy change, the reader can analyze any self-financing combination of policies that is preferred.

Certain combinations of policies have been selected for special analysis.

The policies on minimum wage were, as set out in chapter 5, made self-financing in the sense that price increases met the cost of the minimum wage. It is unlikely, however, that a minimum wage would be introduced in isolation since this would make many people on low incomes worse off in real terms. A combination of policies has therefore been assembled in which the minimum wage is accompanied by a rise in all social security benefits sufficient to protect their real value; such a combination has been considered for a minimum wage of 100 pence per hour for all and for adults.

The seven combined policies considered are:

1. Minimum wage 100 pence for all plus social security increase
2. Minimum wage 100 pence for adults plus social security increase
3. Flat-rate child benefit increase plus NI contribution increase
4. Flat-rate child benefit increase plus income tax rate increase
5. Abolition of married man's tax allowance plus child care allowance
6. Retirement pension increase plus NI contribution increase
7. Retirement pension increase plus income tax rate increase.

In the preceding chapters the analysis has been largely in relation to family incomes, for reasons explained in the introduction. In this chapter effects are also considered in relation to household incomes. The unit of analysis remains the family however and there is a small element of approximation in relation to household income levels; this arises because simulation of the effects of each policy change is made for each family and these have not been combined (for computational reasons) into combined changes for the household. Therefore, family changes are considered in relation to initial household income levels.

The effects of the minimum wage and social security increases are shown in Table 9.2. By contrast with a minimum wage in isolation, which increased the proportion below SB level (Table 5.12), the combined change reduces the proportion below SB level. The effect based on household income is, as shown in Table 9.3,

much less clear cut; there are small reductions in the proportions below SB level
and 140 per cent of SB level but the reductions are much smaller than when family
income is considered.   The reason for this is that many of those with low hourly
earnings who would be affected by a minimum wage are in multi-family households
where the household income level is higher than that of the low-paid person's
family (often, of course, a single person).

Child benefit increases paid for by national insurance contributions or by
an increase in the income tax rate are considered in Tables 9.4 and 9.5.   The
need to finance a child benefit increase reduces its effectiveness in reducing
the proportion below SB level to some extent (see Table 6.4).   Both methods of
financing have similar effects although a rise in the income tax rate has slightly
more effect at the higher income levels.   In relation to both family and
household income levels, the Gini coefficient is reduced and the Atkinson measure
of equality is increased, in relation to family income, when alpha is -0.5 and
-1.0 and, in relation to household income, for all values of alpha.

The next policy combination considered involves the abolition of the married
man's tax allowance and its replacement by a child care allowance.   In this case
the change in child care allowance is adjusted so that the net cost is zero.
This involves a child care allowance at the following rates:

Families with youngest child aged under 5 £12.50 per week.

Families with youngest child aged 5- 10 £6.25 per week.

The mean gains and losses of this combination are shown by income level and type
of family in Table 9.6.   Couples without children inevitably lose but the overall
effect is highly progressive in relation to income levels.   The effects in
relation to family and household income are summarised in Tables 9.7 and 9.8.
There are broadly similar effects to the child benefit increases on the proportions
at low income levels.   The Gini coefficients fall and there is a clear shift
towards greater equality in the Atkinson measure for all three values of alpha
both in relation to family and household incomes.   While the Atkinson measure
is conceptually superior to the Gini coefficient, their correspondence confirms
that this policy combination would increase equality.

The combination of a retirement pension increase and national insurance or income tax increase is analysed in Tables 9.9 and 9.10. Such combinations achieve a marked reduction in the proportions below SB level and, once again, the income tax method of financing is somewhat more progressive. In this case also Gini coefficients fall and, in general, Atkinson measures rise so that there is an increase in equality.

The effect of all the seven measures are summarised in Table 9.11 in terms of their effectiveness in reducing the proportion of families below 140 per cent of SB level, in relation to both family and household income. In terms of family income, the minimum wage for all plus social security increase appears most effective, followed by the pension combinations. In relation to household income the retirement pension combinations appear most effective. It must however be stressed that this final comparison of effectiveness is, like any single summary statistic, very limited. Redistributional effects, as should by now be all too clear, are complex.

Conclusions

This study has attempted to describe the distribution of incomes and to analyse the redistribution of incomes that would result from a number of different policies. It is not the purpose in these conclusions to summarise all of the results in previous chapters which we already described with brevity verging on brusqueness. Rather the intention is to discuss some of the issues involved in analysing redistribution by means of policy simulation.

The description of the distribution of incomes in Part I has followed methods that have now been used in a number of studies. The approach adopted is subject to important qualifications discussed in the Introduction but, it is hoped, it gives as fair a picture as possible of incomes relative to needs.

The simulation of policies has attempted to advance the evaluation of alternative policies. There is sometimes a tendency among proponents of particular policies to assume that they are "a good thing" and that the case for them is self-evident, not requiring any analysis. Such confidence does not alter the fact that choices have to be made; to assist in such choices it may be as well to assess the probable effects in practice of particular policies. While it is often helpful to simulate the possible effects of policies on hypothetical or model families this does not allow any assessment of probable aggregate and distributional effects. To estimate the overall effects of a policy change it is necessary to simulate the effects on some representative sample of the population; it is this that this study has done.

The nature of the effects of certain policies is, to some extent, clear without any simulation; a minimum wage benefits those whose pay is increased; higher child benefits help families with children; increased pensions help the elderly; selective policies such as a tax credit scheme benefit the lowest income levels. It is not surprising - indeed it is reassuring - that computer simulations confirm such effects. Yet, while the nature of the effects may be clear, the size of the effects of different policies on the distribution of incomes cannot be predicted without reference to the initial, existing distribution of incomes. To analyse quantitative effects simulation on the lines described here is essential.

There are four limitations of the simulations presented here which deserve special mention because they offer indications for the development of further more sophisticated simulations in the future.

First, there is the straightforward point that the more recent the data that is used for the simulations the more useful the results will be for policy analysis purposes. Regular collection of data and rapid availability of that data to researchers are necessary if studies such as this are to be more than historical, academic exercises.

Second, there are limitations on the representativeness of the respondents for simulation purposes: there are problems due to bias in the response rate and problems due to the small numbers in certain groups within the sample. Increasing the representativeness of the respondents is a continuing challenge to any survey organisation; those concerned with policy analysis might devote further work to problems of adjusting data for simulating purposes to cope with bias among respondents. To represent accurately small groups - such as disabled people who, in certain age groups, are few in number - further effort might usefully be directed to pooling data from surveys carried out over a number of years.

A third limitation of the simulations, which may be reduced with further work, is in relation to employment responses. Here predicted employment effects have only been incorporated in relation to pensions and illustrative effects considered in relation to a minimum wage. With further work, as more detailed and reliable estimates of employment effects become available, it should be possible to make substantial improvements in the accuracy - and thus usefulness - of policy simulations.

Fourth, this analysis has taken a very simplified approach to the effects of policy changes. While, for example, price effects of a minimum wage and the effects of income tax on increased benefits have been considered, many aspects of the income support system have not been considered. For example, the effects of increased incomes on the take-up or the value of means-tested benefits is ignored. Despite the considerable complexity of the analysis presented here, it is not a full and complete representation of all the ramifications of the British system of taxes and benefits.

A fifth limitation, of a different nature, is that this study has been solely concerned with income distribution. Effects on the equality or inequality of incomes are not all that matter; effects on efficiency of redistributional policies are, in a different way, just as important. Nor should it be forgotten that income and welfare are not the same.

With all these limitations considerable caution and care are necessary in relating the results of the policy simulations presented here to current policy issues. It is clear that there is, therefore, the need and opportunity for much more valuable work in this field. What this study has attempted is, first, to describe how incomes are distributed since an understanding of that distribution is not only important for its own sake but it is also fundamental to the consideration of policies that would redistribute income. Second, the study has attempted to simulate the effects of a number of policies. It is not for the researcher to lay down what distribution or redistribution of incomes is appropriate or necessary, desirable or just. All the researcher can hope to do is to contribute to understanding of the existing distribution of incomes and of what redistribution would result from changes in existing policies. How far that has been achieved is for the reader to judge.

TABLE 9.1

Summary of discrete policy changes

	Exchequer cost £m	Proportion below 140% of SB level	Gini coefficient	Atkinson measure		
				α = -0.5	α = -1.0	α = -2.0
Minimum Wage (No labour demand effect) For all:						
75 pence	-	- 1.3%	- .003	+ .0036	+ .0039	- .0009
100 pence	-	- 2.6%	- .007	+ .0047	+ .0033	- .0060
100 pence with repercussions	-	- 2.8%	- .008	+ .0042	+ .0019	- .0092
For adults:						
75 pence	-	- 0.3%	- .001	+ .0006	+ .0007	- .0004
100 pence	-	- 0.5%	- .001	+ .0004	- .0002	- .0029
100 pence with repercussions	-	- 0.4%	- .001	- .0003	- .0017	- .0054
Child Benefit Increase Flat-rate	1000	- 0.9%	- .002	+ .0008	+ .0002	- .0070
Age-related	1000	- 0.8%	- .002	+ .0005	- .0021	- .0149
Size-related	1000	- 0.9%	- .010	+ .0113	+ .0123	- .0022
Retirement Pension Increase (No labour supply effect)	1000	- 3.4%	- .011	+ .0125	+ .0137	- .0017
NI Contribution Increase	- 1000	+ 0.4%	- .001	+ .0020	+ .0030	+ .0038
Income Tax Rate Increase	- 1000	+ 0.3%	- .002	+ .0026	+ .0029	+ .0017

TABLE 9.2

Effects of minimum wage and social security increase
based on family income

	Initial distribution	Minimum wage	
		100p for all	100p for adults
Proportion below:			
SB level	11.1%	10.4%	10.9%
140% of SB level	32.5%	29.7%	32.0%
5th percentile	0.86	0.86	0.86
Lowest decile	0.98	0.99	0.98
Lower quartile	1.22	1.26	1.22
Median	1.81	1.85	1.83
Upper quartile	2.57	2.56	2.57
Highest decile	3.36	3.31	3.34
95th percentile	3.93	3.87	3.90
Gini coefficient	.280	.271	.278
Atkinson measure			
$\alpha = -0.5$	.8272	.8352	.8293
$\alpha = -1.0$	.7453	.7527	.7471
$\alpha = -2.0$	.3539	.3480	.3511

TABLE 9.3

Effects of minimum wage and social security increase
based on household income

	Initial distribution	Minimum wage	
		100p for all	100p for adults
Proportion below:			
SB level	7.4%	7.3%	7.4%
140% of SB level	26.9%	26.7%	26.8%
5th percentile	0.93	0.93	0.93
Lowest decile	1.04	1.04	1.04
Lower quartile	1.35	1.36	1.36
Median	1.87	1.88	1.88
Upper quartile	2.53	2.52	2.53
Highest decile	3.28	3.24	3.26
95th percentile	3.86	3.81	3.84
Gini coefficient	.255	.251	.253
Atkinson measure			
$\alpha = -0.5$	.8488	.8518	.8503
$\alpha = -1.0$	.7977	.8005	.7991
$\alpha = -2.0$	.6486	.6443	.6462

TABLE 9.4

Effects of child benefit increase and NI contribution
or income tax increase - based on family income

	Initial distribution	Child benefit	
		+ NI contribution	+ income tax
Proportion below:			
SB level	11.1%	10.6%	10.5%
140% of SB level	32.5%	32.3%	32.2%
5th percentile	0.86	0.87	0.87
Lowest decile	0.98	0.99	0.99
Lower quartile	1.22	1.23	1.23
Median	1.81	1.81	1.81
Upper quartile	2.57	2.55	2.55
Highest decile	3.36	3.32	3.31
95th percentile	3.93	3.89	3.88
Gini coefficients	.280	.276	.275
Atkinson measure			
$\alpha = -0.5$	.8272	.8304	.8310
$\alpha = -1.0$	.7453	.7484	.7483
$\alpha = -2.0$	.3539	.3506	.3486

TABLE 9.5

Effects of child benefit increase and NI contribution or income tax increase - based on household income

	Initial distribution	Child benefit	
		+ NI contribution	+ income tax
Proportion below:			
SB level	7.4%	7.0%	7.0%
140% of SB level	26.9%	26.8%	26.7%
5th percentile	0.93	0.95	0.95
Lowest decile	1.04	1.05	1.05
Lower quartile	1.35	1.36	1.36
Median	1.87	1.87	1.87
Upper quartile	2.53	2.52	2.52
Highest decile	3.28	3.25	3.25
95th percentile	3.86	3.83	3.82
Gini coefficient	.255	.252	.251
Atkinson measure			
$\alpha = -0.5$	.8488	.8533	.8537
$\alpha = -1.0$	.7977	.8050	.8049
$\alpha = -2.0$	.6486	.6732	.6692

TABLE 9.6

Effect of abolishing married men's tax allowance and child care allowance
mean gain or loss pence per week

Type of family	Family normal income as % of SB level					
	Under 100	100-	140-	200-	300+	All incomes
Elderly couple	- 73	-135	-277	-329	-333	-200
Couple, no children	-254	-301	-385	-377	-400	-377
Couple, 1 child	+429	+298	+327	+133	-218	+168
Couple, 2 children	+435	+440	+393	+215	+ 94	+305
Couple, 3 children	+505	+453	+319	+234	+285	+329
Couple, 4 children	+432	+407	+303	+235	+416	+340
Couple, 5+ children	- 21	+ 94	+375	+395	+291	+223
Lone parent, 1+ child	+815	+574	+427	+321	+260	+573
Total	+107	+ 50	+ 73	- 41	-194	-

TABLE 9.7

Effect of abolishing married men's tax allowance and
child care allowance - based on family income

	Initial distribution	Adjusted distribution
Proportion below:		
SB level	11.1%	10.7%
140% of SB level	32.5%	31.8%
5th percentile	0.86	0.87
Lowest decile	0.98	0.99
Lower quartile	1.22	1.23
Median	1.81	1.84
Upper quartile	2.57	2.54
Highest decile	3.36	3.30
95th percentile	3.93	3.88
Gini coefficient	.280	.275
Atkinson measure		
$\alpha = -0.5$	.8272	.8334
$\alpha = -1.0$	.7453	.7546
$\alpha = -2.0$	.3539	.3600

TABLE 9.8

Effect of abolishing married men's tax allowance and
child care allowance - based on household income

	Initial distribution	Adjusted distribution
Proportion below:		
SB level	7.4%	7.1%
140% of SB level	26.9%	26.8%
5th percentile	0.93	0.94
Lowest decile	1.04	1.04
Lower quartile	1.35	1.36
Median	1.87	1.87
Upper quartile	2.53	2.51
Highest decile	3.28	3.24
95th percentile	3.86	3.81
Gini coefficient	.255	.250
Atkinson measure		
$\alpha = -0.5$	.8488	.8546
$\alpha = -1.0$	.7977	.8066
$\alpha = -2.0$	.6486	.6769

TABLE 9.9

Effects of retirement pension increase and NI contribution or income tax increase - based on family income

	Initial distribution	Retirement pension	
		+ NI contribution	+ income tax
Proportion below:			
SB level	11.1%	7.9%	7.8%
140% of SB level	32.5%	31.0%	30.8%
5th percentile	0.86	0.89	0.89
Lowest decile	0.98	1.06	1.06
Lower quartile	1.22	1.29	1.29
Median	1.81	1.80	1.81
Upper quartile	2.57	2.53	2.53
Highest decile	3.36	3.31	3.31
95th percentile	3.93	3.88	3.87
Gini coefficient	.280	.268	.267
Atkinson measure			
$\alpha = -0.5$	.8272	.8414	.8421
$\alpha = -1.0$	.7453	.7616	.7616
$\alpha = -2.0$	.3539	.3559	.3538

TABLE 9.10

Effects of retirement pension increase and NI contribution
or income tax increase - based on household income

	Initial distribution	Retirement pension	
		+ NI contribution	+ income tax
Proportion below:			
SB level	7.4%	5.4%	5.4%
140% of SB level	26.9%	25.9%	25.8%
5th percentile	0.93	0.98	0.98
Lowest decile	1.04	1.14	1.14
Lower quartile	1.35	1.38	1.38
Median	1.87	1.86	1.87
Upper quartile	2.53	2.51	2.51
Highest decile	3.28	3.24	3.24
95th percentile	3.86	3.83	3.82
Gini coefficient	.255	.245	.244
Atkinson measure			
$\alpha = -0.5$	.8488	.8607	.8611
$\alpha = -1.0$	.7977	.8130	.8129
$\alpha = -2.0$	.6486	.6635	.6594

TABLE 9.11

Summary of effects of combined policy changes

Percentages

| | Reduction in proportion below 140% of SB level: | |
	Based on family income	Based on household income
Minimum wage 100p for all and social security increase	2.8	0.2
Minimum wage 100p for adults and social security increase	0.5	0.1
Child benefit increase and NI contribution increase	0.2	0.1
Child benefit increase and income tax increase	0.3	0.2
Abolition of married men's tax allowance and child care allowance	0.7	0.1
Retirement pension increase and NI contribution increase	1.5	1.0
Retirement pension increase and income tax increase	1.7	1.1

APPENDIX 1

COMPUTATIONAL METHODOLOGY

by Tony Cornford

The work reported in this paper is based on an analysis of a subset of the 1977 Family Expenditure Survey.

The data used was supplied by the SSRC Survey Archive at Essex University, and subsequently processed on the University of London CDC 7600 Computer, using programs written in FORTRAN and SPSS (Statistical Package for Social Scientists).

The full FES data tape for 1977 contains information on 7198 households containing 19,885 people. In the full survey data tape, information is recorded for a very large number of individual attributes of households and of people, potentially over 700 forms of 'household' expenditure and 1000 forms of 'personal' expenditure. Data on personal and household income and other characteristics is more restricted, but the Survey still potentially offers about 300 different items of information. This vast, and very sparse, data structure is recorded in a variety of variable length records. This raw data tape presents potential secondary analysts with a substantial data processing problem. Most statistical packages require either a rectangular data structure, a data structure in which each case (entity) has exactly the same attributes recorded in a set of fixed format records, or a regular data structure, which permits the definition of relationships between entities each of which has data in a rectangular form e.g., households with from 1 to n people living in them.

The SSRC Survey Archive perform a service to secondary analysts of the FES, in which they subset and reformat this vast and complex data set. The data sets they provide are rectangular with each case representing either one person, or one household. Thus the 1977 FES can be supplied to users as either 7198 cases, one per household, or 19885 cases, one per person. The analyst specifies those variables required. For this study a subset of data based on persons was supplied by the archive, with 185 data items (100 for the person, 85 for the household).

The work reported here is however based on a consideration of the family as the primary entity of interest, and thus the SSRC archive's service did not provide the required data structure. Prior to analysis the data supplied by the archive on a person basis was reformatted into a rectangular structure with one case per family.

This reformatting was done principally by use of the SORT and AGGREGATE procedures of SPSS. The SORT procedure reorders cases, while the AGGREGATE procedure allows information to be generated in various ways for groups of adjacent cases in the sequential file. AGGREGATE allows information drawn from a group of cases to be expressed as maxima, minima, sum, mean etc. The AGGREGATE procedure will function in two possible modes. In the first, data for a group of cases is generated in such a way that it can be added back to each case; this is refered to as the contextual mode. In the second, the procedure effectively generates a new case from the data for a group of individual cases; this is refered to as the true aggregation mode.

To produce the final file of families the following sequence of computer jobs were run.

Job 1 : Sort people into family order

This is required by the AGGREGATE procedure which identifies families or household groups from sets of adjacent cases, e.g. a family will be recorded by the FES in order

      Father

      Mother

      Son aged 19 at work

      Daughter aged 12 at school

Constructing the 2 families represented here demands that in sorting the daughter and son change position.

Job 2 : AGGREGATE family-wide variables and add to each person's record.

(This first attempt at identifying families is used to collect information to be used in cases where the formation of families has to fall back on an imputational procedure)

Job 3 : AGGREGATE household-wide variables and add to each person's record

Job 4 : AGGREGATE people into families, creating a new set of records, one per
family.   At this stage certain data recorded on a household basis, such as
housing expenditure, is apportioned between constituent families in a
household

Analysis is then based on the 'family' set of data.   The FES data as supplied,
provides the information required to identify the members of families.   E.g.
(single person OR married couple) AND (dependent children, if any).

A few anomolies do arise, as in the case of foster children, who the FES coding
scheme treat as independent family units.   The 1977 FES contains 12 foster children
in 8 households (10 families).

A further complication arises in the case of a family in which one of the
adults is temporarily absent - in which case no data is available on the absent
person.

Following the family creation process 72 families were rejected from the sample
on the basis of

Rejection criteria	Families
Foster children present in household	10
Bad data on tape	1
Adult temporarily away from household	44
Head of family unit 15 years old	4
Household income less than £0	13
	72

leaving a final file of 9152 families.

The family is considered the most suitable entity on which to base these
analyses and simulations since most social security policies operate at the level
of an inner family unit made up of a head and spouse and dependent children.
However, the exact definition of families may vary as a study moves from task to
task.

Specifically the problems of family identification arise in 3 main areas:

(1) Administrative systems modify and adapt the concept.   Thus the child benefit
     system recognises 16-18 year old children as dependent on their parents
     if in secondary education, while the tax system may recognise them as
     dependent whatever type of education they were in.

(2) The family, as a unit of shared levels of living, will always be a combination
     of biological and social relationships.   Foster children are a case in point,
     as are the not infrequent cases of grandparents bringing up children, and
     cohabitation.

(3) The family can be spatially difuse, as for example, dependent children away at
     university and families where the father works temporarily away from home.

In using a survey such as the FES for this type of secondary analysis, and in
seeking to redefine the data structure of it, the analyst is to a large extent
dependent on the sampling and coding scheme used in the primary survey.

In the case of the FES the coding scheme does record enough data at least to
identify most family formation conflicts, but there are occurences in which there
is not enough data to proceed.

In handling this situation the data restructuring fell back on an imputational
procedure.   One example is the recording of students away at university.   The
survey records such people on a household basis, and not a family basis: If more
than one family was present, the family to which the student most probably belonged
was selected (in no case was there any apparent doubt).

A major proportion of the work reported here is policy simulation.   The style
of analysis used may be termed 'microcosmic' modelling.   Analysis is based on
micro data.   A sample of micro units is used to investigate the status and simulate
the responses of the whole population of micro units, in this case families.   Microcosmic models as used here are thus models of multiple aspect of large systems
constructed by use of a sample of the constituent elements of the system, creating
a microcosm, hence 'microcosmic'.

A system modelled in this way is considered to consist of a number of a single homogeneous type of unit, in this case the family. The number of people in the family and their personal characteristics are attributes of the family.

In simulating policy changes it is desired to investigate the aggregate status and response of all families to some policy change. The emphasis on distributional issues demands that, although a particular policy operates only on one section of the community, the simulation results must be presented in terms of the resulting overall distribution. The simulation technique used may require up to three separate stages, each supported by a suitable model, and realised by the computer software used.

Stage 1 : Some attributes of the family are changed in line with the policy

Stage 2 : The family make some response to the policy

Stage 3 : The policy produces some system-wide feedback.

Examples of these 3 stages are

	Minimum wage (chapter 5)	Retirement pension (chapter 7)
1. Family attributes	Change hourly wage rate Compute new net earnings	Change pension rate
2. Family response	-	Elderly workers withdraw from labour market
3. System feedback	Change in price level Generated unemployment	-

In general, using SPSS gives rise to problems only at the third stage, requiring manual iteration of jobs.

In the type of simulation reported here, the families, as system entities, respond only to changes in the general systems environment, or to exogeneous changes imposed on them. They do not react dynamically with any other individual system entity. For example, the effect of raising pensions on labour supply is simulated only as the direct effect on individual families. Two families living in the same household do not interact in their responses.

For certain simulations a limited amount of static entity interaction is possible since the database does allow families to have some information about those with whom they share households.   More generally this information is used to provide a context to view results and not as a parameter of family response models.

6282222822622226282262822

APPENDIX 2

CONSTRUCTION OF VARIABLES

FES CODES HAVE BEEN USED AND THEIR NUMBERS RETAINED BUT PREFIXES HAVE BEEN ADDED AS FOLLOWS:

H – HEAD OF FAMILY

S – SPOUSE

AG – AGGREGATE OF ALL CHILDREN IN FAMILY UNIT

VARIABLES HAVE BEEN CONSTRUCTED USING THE FOLLOWING PREFIXES:

F – FAMILY

H – HOUSEHOLD

```
COMMENT         CALCULATION OF SB LEVEL    AND TYPEFU
COMPUTE         KIDS=0
IF              (SA001 GT 0)COUPLE=2
IF              (HA005 GT 65)ELDERLY=1
IF              (HA005 GT 60 AND HA004 EQ 2)ELDERLY=1
COMPUTE         FSBLEV=15700
IF              (SA001 GT 0) FSBLEV=FSBLEV + 9150
DO REPEAT       XAGE=AD1,AD2,AD3,AD4,AD5,AD6,AD7,AD8,AD9,AD10,AD11,AD12/
IF              (XAGE GT 0 AND LT 5) FSBLEV=FSBLEV + 3600
IF              (XAGE GE 5 AND LE 10)FSBLEV=FSBLEV + 4350
IF              (XAGE GE 11 AND LE 12)FSBLEV=FSBLEV+ 5350
IF              (XAGE GE 13 AND LE 15)FSBLEV=FSBLEV+ 6500
IF              (XAGE GE 16 AND LE 17) FSBLEV=FSBLEV + 7800
IF              (XAGE GE 18) FSBLEV=FSBLEV + 12600
IF              (XAGE GT 0)KIDS=KIDS+1
END REPEAT
COMPUTE         FSBSHORT=FSBLEV-3000
IF              (SA001 GT 0)FSBSHORT=FSBSHORT-1200
IF              (WEEK GE 43)FSBSHORT=FSBSHORT*1.140
IF              (WEEK GE 43)FSBLEV=1.140*FSBLEV
COMPUTE         MSBLEV=15700*SINGS+24850*COUP+3600*(AGE1+AGE2)+4350*(AGE3+AGE4)+
                5350*AGE5+6500*AGE6+7800*AGE7+12600*AGE8
IF              (WEEK GE 43)MSBLEV=MSBLEV*1.140
IF              (COUPLE EQ 2)TYPEFU=4+KIDS
IF              (KIDS GE 5)TYPEFU=9
IF              (COUPLE EQ 0)TYPEFU=10+HA004
IF              (COUPLE EQ 0 AND KIDS GT 0)TYPEFU=10
IF              (ELDERLY EQ 1 AND COUPLE EQ 2)TYPEFU=1
IF              (ELDERLY EQ 1 AND COUPLE EQ 0)TYPEFU=1+HA004
COMPUTE         FINDS=1
IF              (COUPLE EQ 2)FINDS=2
COMPUTE         FINDS=FINDS+KIDS
.
COMMENT         CALCULATION OF INCOMES RELATIVE TO SB
COMPUTE         FNREL=(FNNET-(SHARE*(NETHSG+MORTINT)))/FSBLEV
COMPUTE         FCREL=(FCNET-(SHARE*(NETHSG+MORTINT)))/FSBLEV
COMPUTE         MREL=(P399-NETHSG-MORTINT)/MSBLEV
COMPUTE         MTRANS=(MREL-FNREL)*FSBLEV
COMPUTE         GFNREL=100*FNREL
COMPUTE         GFCREL=100*FCREL
COMPUTE         GMREL=100*MREL
RECODE          GFNREL TO GMREL         (0=0)(1 THRU 89.9=1)(89.9 THRU 99.9=2 )
                (99.9 THRU 119.9=3  )(119.9 THRU 139.9=4  )(139.9 THRU 199.9=5)
                (199.9 THRU 299.9=6  )(299.9 THRU 499.9=7  )(499.9 THRU HI=8)
VALUE LABELS    TYPEFU (1)ELDERLY COUPLE(2)ELDERLY MAN(3)ELDERLY WOMAN(4)COUPLE
                (5)MC 1 CHILD(6)MC 2 CHILDREN(7)MC 3 CHILDREN(8)MC 4 CHILDREN
                (9)MC 5+ CHILDREN(10)ONE PARENT+CHILD(11)LONE MAN(12)LONE WOMAN
..
```

```
COMMENT      FAMILY AND HOUSEHOLD INCOMES
COMPUTE      SHARE=(HP051+SP051)/(P344-P274-P277)
COMPUTE      FNGR=HP051+SP051+HP046+SP046+AGP051
COMPUTE      FNGR =FNGR +SHARE*(P277+P274)
COMPUTE      FCGR=HP053+SP053+HP046+HP046+AGP053
COMPUTE      FCGR =FCGR +SHARE*(P277+P274)
COMPUTE      FNNET=FNGR - (HP075+HP076+HP079+HP029+SP075+SP076+SP079+SP029)
COMPUTE      FCNET=FCGR - (HP075+HP076+HP079+HP029+SP075+SP076+SP079+SP029)
COMPUTE      MNNET=P399-HP289
COMPUTE      MCNET=P399-P344+P352-HP289

COMMENT      COMBINING COUPLES INCOMES
COMPUTE      FTAX=HP079+SP079
COMPUTE      FNICON=HP075+HP076+SP075+SP076
COMPUTE      HNEARN=HP007+HP014+HP037+HP046+HP047
COMPUTE      SNEARN=SP007+SP014+SP037+SP046+SP047
COMPUTE      HCEARN=HNEARN-HP007+HP004
COMPUTE      SCEARN=SNEARN-SP007+SP004
COMPUTE      FFIS=HP013+SP013
COMPUTE      FUB=HP022+SP022
COMPUTE      FSIKII=HP023+SP023
COMPUTE      FSUPAL=HP025+SP025
COMPUTE      FFAM=HU337+SU337
COMPUTE      FRETPENS=HU338+SU338
COMPUTE      FWIDPENS=HU339+SU339
COMPUTE      FDISPENS=HU340+SU340
COMPUTE      FSSLONG=HP031+SP031
COMPUTE      FSSSHRT=HP030+SP030
COMPUTE      FINVALID=HP032+SP032
COMPUTE      FINVY=HP048+SP048
COMPUTE      FPENS=HP049+SP049
COMPUTE      FOTHERY=HP050+SP050
COMPUTE      MORTINT=U131+U132+U133+U134+U135+U151+U152+U153+U154+U155
COMPUTE      NETHSG =P281+P282+P283+P284+P285+P286

COMMENT      CALCULATING NET INCOME USING TAKE HOME PAY
COMPUTE      HCNET=HP002+HP012+HP037+HP046+HP047+HP048+HP049+HP050+HP079-(
             HP077-HP078)
COMPUTE      SCNET=SP002+SP012+SP037+SP046+SP047+SP048+SP049+SP050+SP079-(
             SP077-SP078)
```

BIBLIOGRAPHY

B. Abel-Smith and P. Townsend: The Poor and the Poorest, Bell, 1965.

A.B. Atkinson: 'On the Measurement of Inequality', Journal of Economic Theory, Vol.2, 1972.

W. Beckerman: 'The Impact of Income Maintenance Payments on Poverty in Britain'. Economic Journal, Vol.86, 1979.

C.V. Brown: The Impact of Tax Changes on Income Distribution, Institute for Fiscal Studies, 1972.

Department of Employment, New Earnings Survey 1977, HMSO, 1977.

G. Fiegehen, S. Lansley and A. Smith: Poverty and Progress in Britain 1953-73, Cambridge University Press 1977.

M. Friedman: Capitalism and Freedom, University of Chicago Press, 1962.

C. Greenhalgh: 'Participation and hours of work for married women in Great Britain', Oxford Economic Papers, Vol.32, 1980.

W.F.F. Kemsley, R.U. Redpath and M. Holmes: Family Expenditure Survey Handbook, HMSO, 1980.

R. Layard, M. Barton and A. Zabalza: 'Married women's participation and hours', Economica, Vol.47, 1980.

R. Layard, D. Piachaud and M. Stewart: The Causes of Poverty, Royal Commission on the Distribution of Income and Wealth, Background Paper No.5, HMSO, 1978.

D. Piachaud: The Cost of a Child, Child Poverty Action Group, 1979.

C. Sandford, C. Pond and R. Walker (eds): 'Taxation and Social Policy', Heinemann, 1980.

P. Townsend: Poverty in the United Kingdom, Allen Lane, 1979.

A. Zabalza and D. Piachaud: 'Social Security and the Elderly, A Simulation of Policy Changes', LSE, Centre for Labour Economics, Discussion Paper No. 61, 1980. (Forthcoming in Journal of Public Economics).

Proposals for a Tax-Credit System, Cmnd. 5116, HMSO, 1972.